# A HERO'S GUIDE TO
# WARRIORS

## DEBORAH MURRELL

QEB Publishing

Library of Congress Cataloging-in-Publication Data

Murrell, Deborah Jane, 1963-
Samurai / by Deborah Murrell.
 p. cm. -- (QEB warriors)
 Includes index.
 ISBN 978-1-59566-734-2 (hardcover)
 1. Samurai--Juvenile literature. 2. Military art and science--Japan--Juvenile literature. 3. Japan--History, Military--Juvenile literature. I. Title.
 DS827.S3M875 2010
 355.00952--dc22
             2009003545

Murrell, Deborah Jane, 1963-
Knight / by Deborah Murrell.
 p. cm. -- (QEB warriors)
 Includes index.
 ISBN 978-1-59566-735-9 (hardcover)
 1. Knights and knighthood--Juvenile literature. 2. Civilization, Medieval--Juvenile literature. I. Title.
 CR4513.M874 2010
 940.1--dc22
             2009003544

Murrell, Deborah Jane, 1963-
Greek warrior / by Deborah Murrell.
 p. cm. -- (QEB warriors)
 Includes index.
 ISBN 978-1-59566-759-5 (hardcover)
 1. Military art and science--Greece--History--Juvenile literature. 2. Soldiers--Greece--History. 3. Greece--History, Military--To 146 B.C.--Juvenile literature. I. Title.

U33.M876 2010
355.00938--dc22
             2009003542

Murrell, Deborah Jane, 1963-
Gladiator / written by Deborah Murrell.
 p. cm. -- (QEB warriors)
 Includes index.
 ISBN 978-1-59566-736-6 (hardcover)
 1. Gladiators--Juvenile literature. I. Title.
 GV35.M87 2010
 796.8'0937--dc22
             2009003540

Author Deborah Murrell
Consultant Philip Steele
Editor Eve Marleau
Designer and Picture
   Researcher Andrew McGovern
Illustrator Peter Dennis

Publisher Steve Evans
Creative Director Zeta Davies
Managing Editor Amanda Askew

Printed in Singapore

The words in **bold** are explained in the glossary on page 116.

# CONTENTS

# GREEK WARRIOR

# CONTENTS

# WHAT WAS A HOPLITE?

A hoplite was a type of ancient Greek soldier. Hoplites fought on foot and were the most important men in Greek armies.

## Military life

Soldiers, including hoplites, in ancient Greece did not usually belong to a full-time army. They had jobs when they were not at war.

➤ Most hoplites came from wealthy families who could afford to buy the weapons and armor they needed.

# SPARTANS

After 700 BC, the southern Greek city of Sparta began to take over the surrounding region called Lakonia. The Spartans made the people from the villages do their work, such as farming. The Spartans became full-time soldiers. Soon they were the most feared army in ancient Greece.

## Poorer soldiers

Men from poorer families also fought in Greek armies. They could not afford the weapons and armor to become hoplites, so they fought as **archers** or with **slings** and stones.

> *Poorer soldiers often fought with long-distance weapons, such as stones or bows and arrows.*

# WHEN DID HOPLITES LIVE?

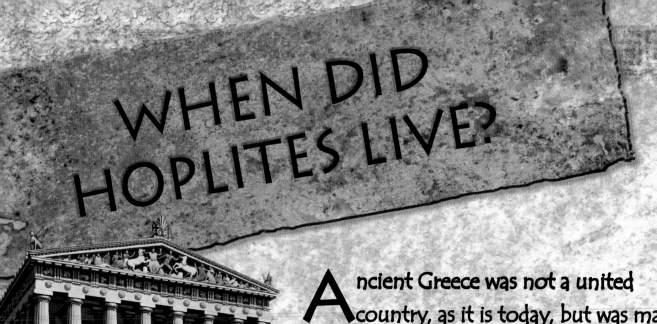

**A**ncient Greece was not a united country, as it is today, but was made up of city-states. Armies often fought over territories. Hoplites were the main force in Greek armies between 600 and 300 BC.

## Athens versus Sparta

Athens and Sparta were two of the strongest city-states in ancient Greece. Athens made a lot of money by trading, and it had a large navy to protect its sea routes. Sparta had a very strong land army, based around its hoplites.

▲ *The Parthenon was the temple of Athena. This goddess was believed to protect the city of Athens.*

## Greek armies

In ancient times, warriors with shields and spears often fought as a line formation to break through enemy front lines. The Greek city-states perfected this way of fighting, which they called a **phalanx**.

ILLYRIA

MACEDONIA

THRACE

Black Sea

*Athens and Sparta were two of the most powerful city-states.*

Byzantium •
Sea of Marmara

CHALCIDICE

EPIRUS

THESSALY

Corfu

PHRYGIA

MYSIA

Aegean Sea

ANATOLIA

AETOLIA

LOCRIS

PHOCIS **Delphi**
•
BOEOTIA

ATTICA

ACHAEA

LYDIA

Ionian Sea

**Corinth**
•
**Athens**
•

Peloponnese

CARIA

IONIA

Cyclades

LYCIA

Dodecanese

LACONIA

**Sparta**
•

Rhodes

*Greek soldiers fought off Persian invaders at the Battle of Plataea in 479 BC.*

# AESCHYLUS
## (c.525–456 BC)

Aeschylus was one of the greatest Greek writers. He fought in a famous battle at Marathon, near Athens. This is mentioned on his grave, but his plays are not!

# TRAINING TO BE A HOPLITE

Hoplites throughout ancient Greece fought in much the same way, so they learned similar techniques. Hoplites were trained to work together as a team in a phalanx.

## Boarding school

At about seven years old, Spartan boys were sent to boarding school for training to be hoplites. They learned many skills, including how to hunt and dance. They were not given much food, so they had to look after themselves. This often meant stealing from the other boys. The boys were not punished for stealing, but for being caught doing it.

*Spartan boys exercised to stay strong and fit.*

# Daily practice

Activities such as athletics contests helped hoplites gain the skills and strength they needed for battles. Spartan boys also had to learn poems by heart and read the work of great Greek philosophers, or thinkers.

*Spartan boys practiced with wooden spears and shields and were carefully watched over by their teachers.*

## WARRIOR WISDOM

At about 20 years old, Spartan men became members of a dining club. This was a special club where a small group of men would eat together. The club taught the men to rely on and trust each other. It was only after training and club membership that a man became a hoplite.

# WEAPONS AND ARMOR

Helmet

**T**he most important part of a hoplite's armor was his shield. In the battle formation, or phalanx, the shield protected the hoplite holding it and the man to his left.

## Shields

Hoplites carried large, round shields, made of wood or **bronze**. Shields were carried on the left arm so the right arm was free for fighting. The fighting arm was also protected by the shield of the man to the right in a phalanx.

Chest armor

➤*The length of the hoplites' spears kept the enemy at a safe distance in the early stages of battle.*

Greave

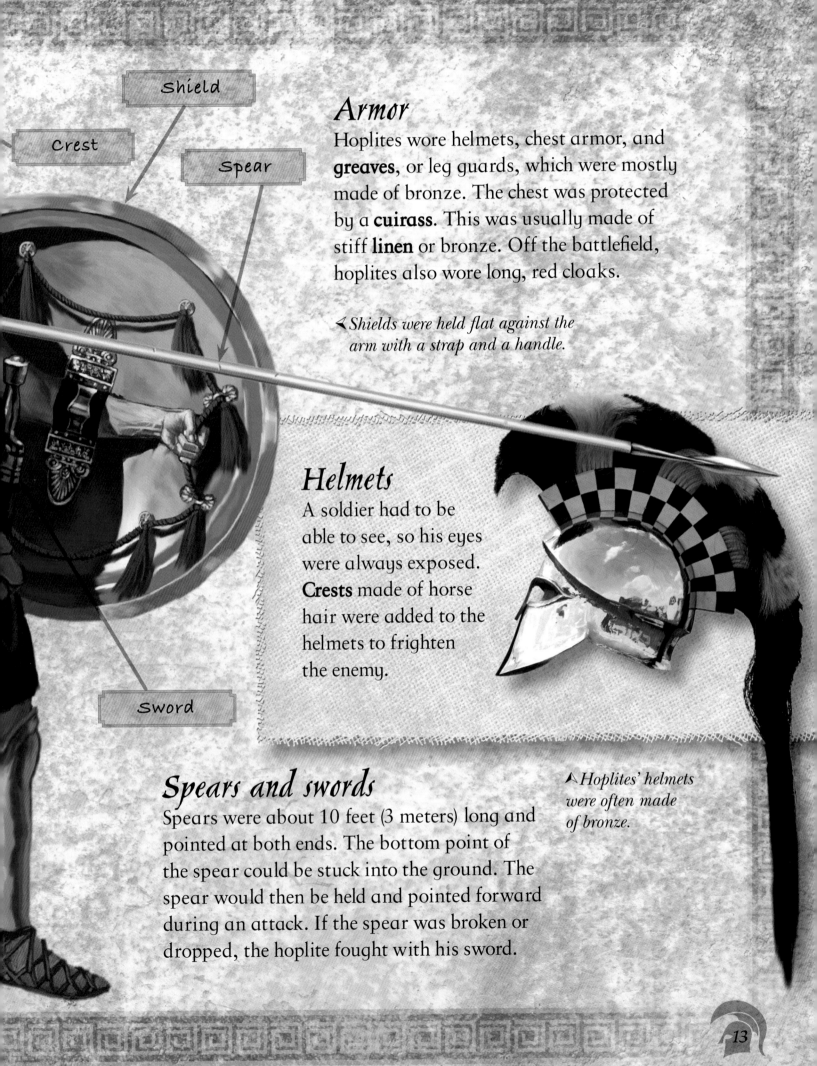

Shield

Crest

Spear

Sword

## Armor

Hoplites wore helmets, chest armor, and **greaves**, or leg guards, which were mostly made of bronze. The chest was protected by a **cuirass**. This was usually made of stiff **linen** or bronze. Off the battlefield, hoplites also wore long, red cloaks.

*◁ Shields were held flat against the arm with a strap and a handle.*

## Helmets

A soldier had to be able to see, so his eyes were always exposed. **Crests** made of horse hair were added to the helmets to frighten the enemy.

*△ Hoplites' helmets were often made of bronze.*

## Spears and swords

Spears were about 10 feet (3 meters) long and pointed at both ends. The bottom point of the spear could be stuck into the ground. The spear would then be held and pointed forward during an attack. If the spear was broken or dropped, the hoplite fought with his sword.

# WAR MACHINES

For hoplites, the main tactic was to fight in a phalanx. Battles were often won by pushing the enemy off the battlefield. However, other kinds of tactics were also used.

*➤ Greek ships usually had both sails and oars. In battle, or if there was no wind, men used the oars to power the ship.*

*⋀ Battering rams were used to break down walls. Catapults threw torches into the city.*

## Under siege

**Sieges,** or attacks on cities, were not very common in ancient Greece. When they did happen, various tactics were used. Hoplites sometimes used ladders, for example, to climb up enemy walls. However, the best weapons in a siege were large machines, such as **battering rams** and **catapults**.

## All at sea

The most useful kind of warship in ancient Greece was called a **trireme**. Its name means "three oars," as it had three banks of oars on each side. It also had a battering ram on the front. Triremes did not carry many soldiers—the ship itself was the main weapon.

## SHIP SHAKER

Many Greek cities were on the coast. In 214 BC, after the time of hoplites, a scientist named Archimedes invented a useful machine. A large hook was lowered from a crane and hooked under the enemy ship. Oxen pulled the ship out of the water. When the rope was released, the ship crashed into the water and sank.

# WAR WITH PERSIA

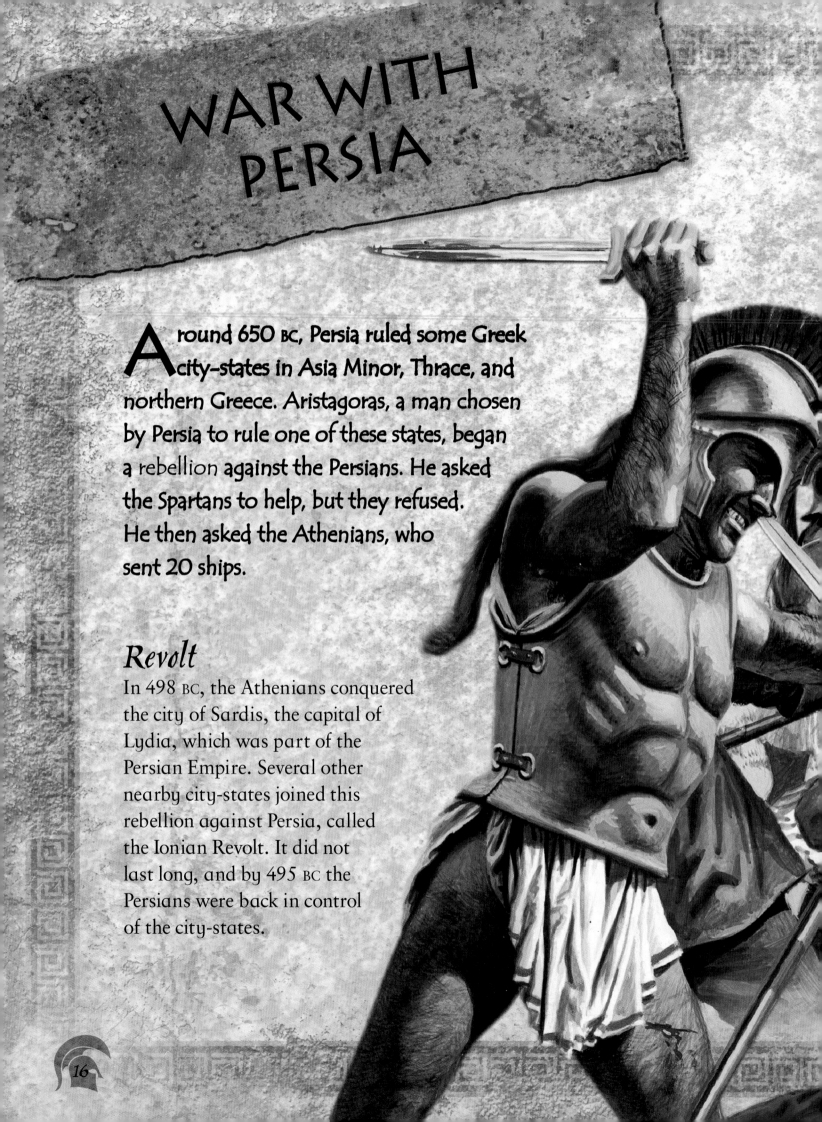

Around 650 BC, Persia ruled some Greek city-states in Asia Minor, Thrace, and northern Greece. Aristagoras, a man chosen by Persia to rule one of these states, began a rebellion against the Persians. He asked the Spartans to help, but they refused. He then asked the Athenians, who sent 20 ships.

## Revolt

In 498 BC, the Athenians conquered the city of Sardis, the capital of Lydia, which was part of the Persian Empire. Several other nearby city-states joined this rebellion against Persia, called the Ionian Revolt. It did not last long, and by 495 BC the Persians were back in control of the city-states.

## The Battle of Marathon

The Persians did not forget the part Athens had played in the Ionian Revolt and, in 490 BC, they attacked Athens. The two armies met at Marathon, north of Athens. The Athenians were led by Miltiades, a soldier who had fought in the Persian army and knew how to beat them. He led the Athenians to victory.

▼ *Greeks and Persians fought a long and bloody battle at Marathon, near Athens.*

### WARRIOR WISDOM

After the Battle of Marathon, a runner was sent to take the news of victory to Athens. He ran the 25 miles (41 kilometers) in armor. It is thought that he died just after passing on his message. Marathons are named after this event.

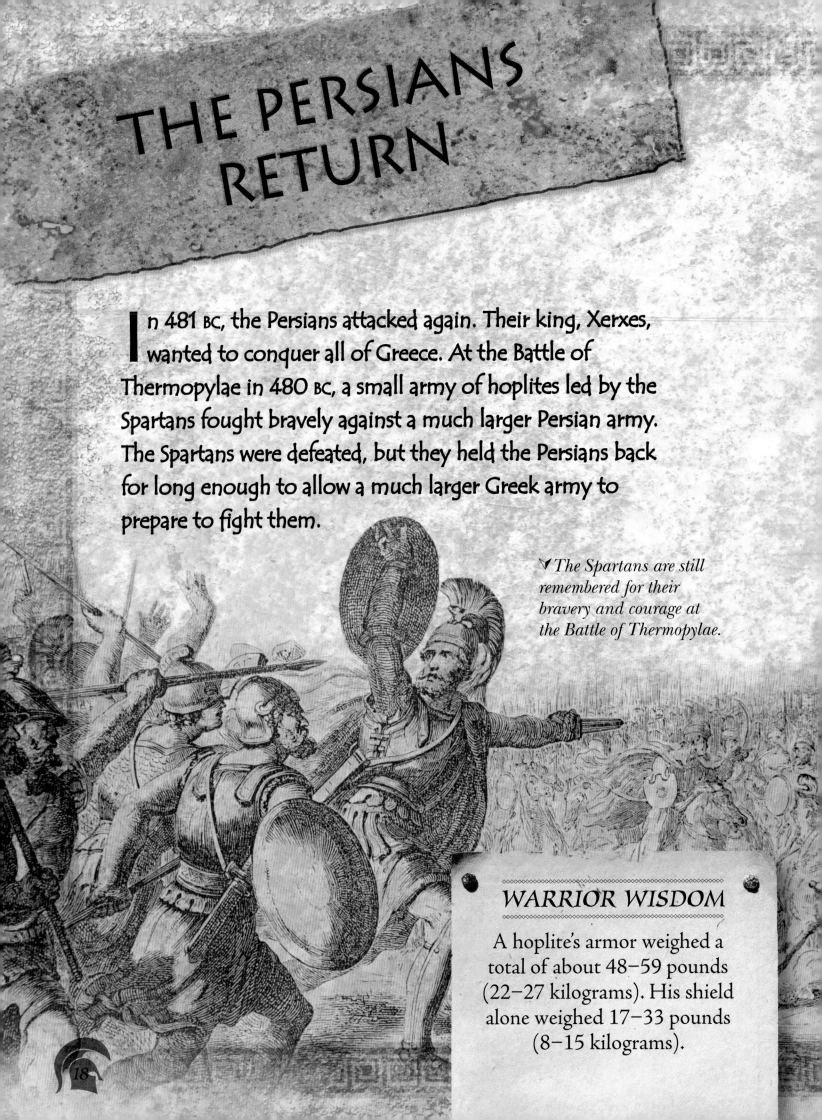

# THE PERSIANS RETURN

In 481 BC, the Persians attacked again. Their king, Xerxes, wanted to conquer all of Greece. At the Battle of Thermopylae in 480 BC, a small army of hoplites led by the Spartans fought bravely against a much larger Persian army. The Spartans were defeated, but they held the Persians back for long enough to allow a much larger Greek army to prepare to fight them.

*⌄The Spartans are still remembered for their bravery and courage at the Battle of Thermopylae.*

## WARRIOR WISDOM

A hoplite's armor weighed a total of about 48–59 pounds (22–27 kilograms). His shield alone weighed 17–33 pounds (8–15 kilograms).

## The Battle of Salamis

When Xerxes and his army came to attack a month after Thermopylae, the Athenians had a fleet of ships and were ready for them. In a battle off the island of Salamis, the Greeks beat the Persian fleet.

## Peace at last

Although they had defeated the Persians, many Greeks feared they might return. The Athenians' victory meant many of the other city-states relied on Athens' ships to protect them. This made Athens very powerful. Sparta was also powerful, and the Spartans became jealous and suspicious of Athens.

▷ The Battle of Salamis was the battle that won the Persian War for the Greeks.

# DEFEAT OF THE SPARTANS

After the Persian Wars, the city-states of ancient Greece continued to fight. Athens and Sparta led groups of city-states called leagues. Each league wanted to take control of more land. This fight for control was called the Peloponnesian War.

*▽ Sometimes both sails and oars were needed to control a ship.*

## War between states

The Peloponnesian War began in 431 BC. At first, the Delian League, led by Athens' army, won many battles with their strong navy. Eventually, they surrendered to the Peloponnesian League, led by Sparta, in 404 BC.

## Battle of Leuctra

Fighting between city-states did not stop. One of the most important battles took place at Leuctra in 371 BC between Sparta and Thebes. The Spartan hoplites were arranged in phalanxes of 8–12 lines, with the strongest fighters on the right. The Thebans attacked on the right with **cavalry** and 50 lines of hoplites. The Spartans, seeing their strongest men beaten, left the battlefield.

*▼ Before a battle, hoplites carried their spears pointing upward.*

### PHILIP II
### (c.525–456 BC)
The Thebans did not have long to enjoy their victory. Greece was soon invaded by the army of Philip II of Macedonia, in the north of Greece.

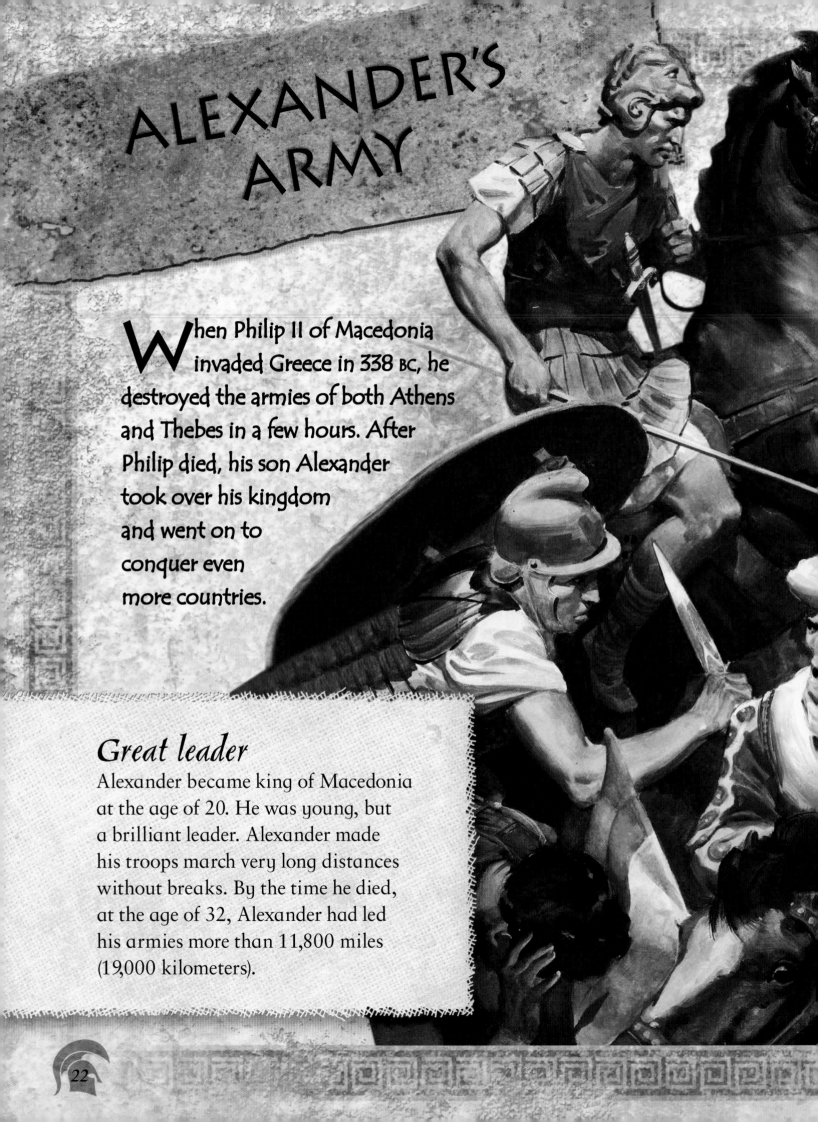

# ALEXANDER'S ARMY

When Philip II of Macedonia invaded Greece in 338 BC, he destroyed the armies of both Athens and Thebes in a few hours. After Philip died, his son Alexander took over his kingdom and went on to conquer even more countries.

## Great leader

Alexander became king of Macedonia at the age of 20. He was young, but a brilliant leader. Alexander made his troops march very long distances without breaks. By the time he died, at the age of 32, Alexander had led his armies more than 11,800 miles (19,000 kilometers).

## The cavalry

Philip II and Alexander had cavalry as well as foot soldiers in their armies. The cavalry were called hetairoi. This means "companions."

◄ The hetairoi often rode ahead of the foot soldiers.

◄ Alexander the Great's horse, Bucephalus, was said to be an unusually strong and courageous horse in battle.

### WARRIOR WISDOM

Alexander rode a horse called Bucephalus into battle. It was said the horse was offered to Philip II but could not be tamed. Alexander realized that Bucephalus was frightened of his own shadow, and was able to tame him.

# MACEDONIAN WEAPONS AND ARMOR

The army of ancient northern Greece, or Macedonia, was one of the greatest in the world. Philip II created this army, and Alexander made it even stronger.

## Sarissa

Macedonian soldiers carried a **sarissa**, or long spear. They could easily stab an enemy from far away. Macedonian soldiers fought in a phalanx, like the ancient Greeks. The first few rows held out their sarissas, but soldiers who were further back held theirs upward, to keep them out of the way.

⌃Sarissas looked like long spears and had sharp points at either end.

◀ *The cavalry carried spears and a sword into battle.*

## Riding high

The hetairoi carried a spear and wore many kinds of armor. The armor was made of linen and leather, with pieces of metal, like scales, attached. Some wore full metal breastplates to protect the chest.

## Armor

Macedonian soldiers wore body armor made of leather. Their shields were smaller and lighter than those of Greek hoplites, which may have made it easier to move.

◀ *Short swords were better for close fighting.*

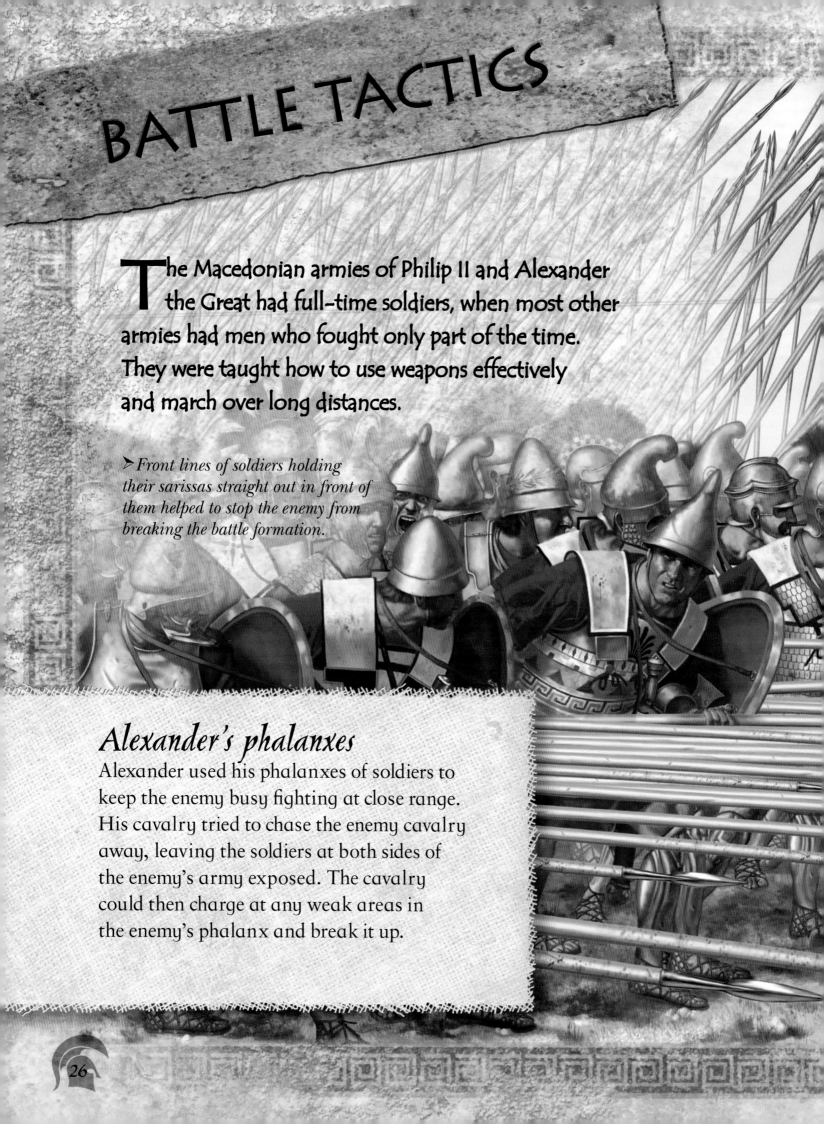

# BATTLE TACTICS

The Macedonian armies of Philip II and Alexander the Great had full-time soldiers, when most other armies had men who fought only part of the time. They were taught how to use weapons effectively and march over long distances.

> *Front lines of soldiers holding their sarissas straight out in front of them helped to stop the enemy from breaking the battle formation.*

## Alexander's phalanxes

Alexander used his phalanxes of soldiers to keep the enemy busy fighting at close range. His cavalry tried to chase the enemy cavalry away, leaving the soldiers at both sides of the enemy's army exposed. The cavalry could then charge at any weak areas in the enemy's phalanx and break it up.

## In the thick of things

Both Philip II's and Alexander the Great's armies had men who ran out in front of the main army, using weapons such as bows, slings, and **javelins** to try and break up the lines.

### WARRIOR WISDOM

Alexander's men marched much faster than most armies. Sometimes an enemy surrendered just because they had not expected Alexander to arrive quite so quickly.

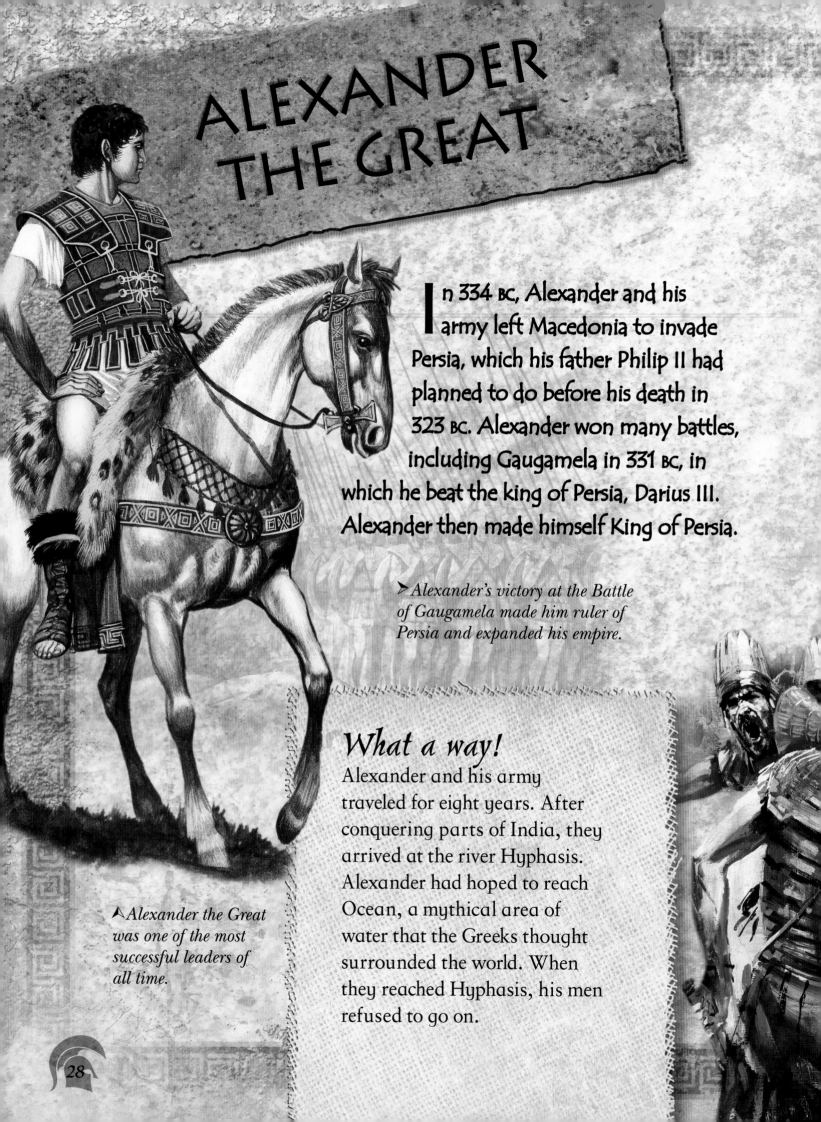

# ALEXANDER THE GREAT

In 334 BC, Alexander and his army left Macedonia to invade Persia, which his father Philip II had planned to do before his death in 323 BC. Alexander won many battles, including Gaugamela in 331 BC, in which he beat the king of Persia, Darius III. Alexander then made himself King of Persia.

➤ *Alexander's victory at the Battle of Gaugamela made him ruler of Persia and expanded his empire.*

➤ *Alexander the Great was one of the most successful leaders of all time.*

## What a way!

Alexander and his army traveled for eight years. After conquering parts of India, they arrived at the river Hyphasis. Alexander had hoped to reach Ocean, a mythical area of water that the Greeks thought surrounded the world. When they reached Hyphasis, his men refused to go on.

## No heir

Alexander ruled Egypt, western and central Asia, and a small part of India. He built a city called Alexandria, named after himself, in Egypt. He had a short life, but he was famous all over the world. Alexander did not have an official **heir** to rule the kingdom after his death. It was divided up into several sections, each ruled by one of his strongest **generals**.

◮ *The Pharos lighthouse was built between 285–247 BC, on an island just off Alexandria, in Egypt.*

### WARRIOR WISDOM

Before the Battle of Gaugamela, there was an **eclipse** of the moon. Darius III thought the eclipse was a sign that a warrior from the west was going to rule for eight years. He was right.

# THE DECLINE OF ANCIENT GREECE

Greece itself soon became divided once again. The growing power in the Mediterranean was Rome. Its empire spread far and wide, and Greece was conquered by 146 BC.

*▼Many buildings, such as those in the Forum in Rome, are in the style of Greek architecture.*

## Greek influence

Alexander spread Greek culture around Asia. He built many cities in which the people followed the Greek way of life. The period from Alexander's death to the beginning of the Roman Empire in 141 BC is known as the **Hellenistic Age**, after the Greeks' name for themselves, Hellenes. The Romans appreciated and learned a lot from Greek culture. The world had moved on, but it was taking Greek ideas with it.

➤ *Life in ancient Greece did not change much after the Romans conquered it in 141 BC.*

## Just another day

For most people, the decline of ancient Greece did not make much of a difference to everyday life. Some Greek warriors fought as soldiers for the Roman army, and many others returned to the jobs they had done when they were not fighting.

# GLADIATOR

# CONTENTS

# WHAT WAS A GLADIATOR?

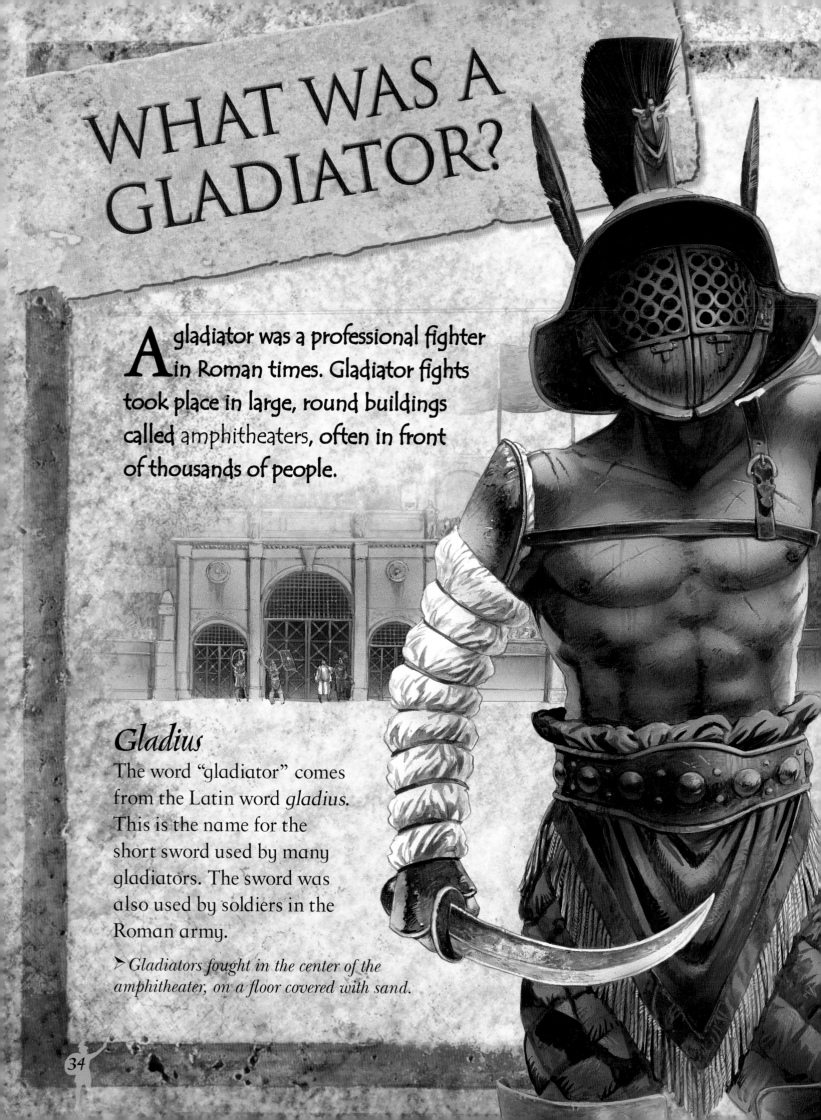

**A** gladiator was a professional fighter in Roman times. Gladiator fights took place in large, round buildings called amphitheaters, often in front of thousands of people.

## Gladius

The word "gladiator" comes from the Latin word *gladius*. This is the name for the short sword used by many gladiators. The sword was also used by soldiers in the Roman army.

➤ *Gladiators fought in the center of the amphitheater, on a floor covered with sand.*

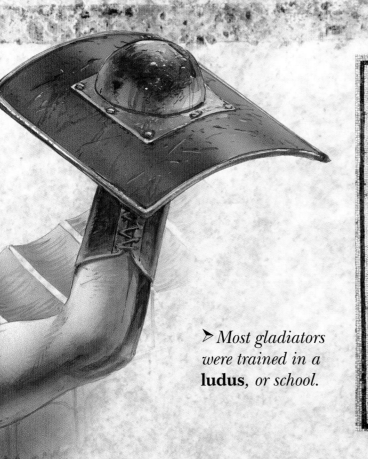

> Most gladiators were trained in a **ludus**, or school.

## Who were gladiators?

Gladiators were mainly men who were slaves, criminals, or prisoners of war. They were kept locked up and forced to fight. If a gladiator was very good and won many fights, he might be freed and, sometimes, earn money.

## Female gladiators

A few women fought as gladiators. Most Romans did not approve of women in the **arena**, so they were not often seen there. **Emperor** Nero enjoyed watching female gladiators. He even made some noble women fight each other.

> Emperor Nero was a supporter of the gladiator games.

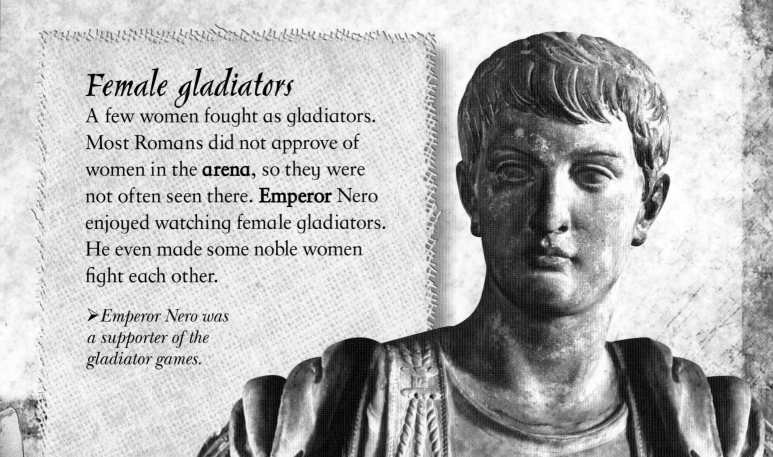

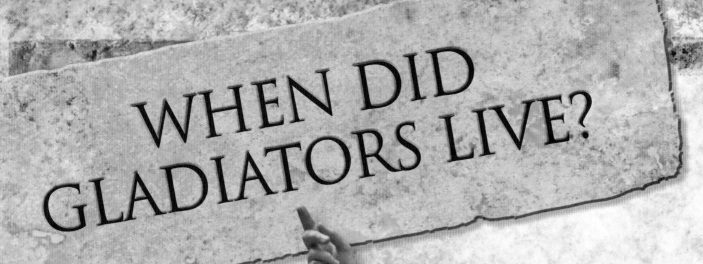

# WHEN DID GLADIATORS LIVE?

The first recorded gladiator fight among Romans took place in ancient Rome in 264 BC, in the *Forum Boarium*, or cattle market. It was part of the funeral for an important Roman citizen.

*◄ Emperor Augustus lived from 63 BC to AD 14.*

## Ancient Rome

Rome was originally ruled by kings who were advised by **senators**. The last king, Tarquinius, was removed in 510 BC. Senators then ruled Rome as a **republic** and tried to conquer the land around it. Army generals became very powerful. In 49 BC, the general Julius Caesar took control of the Roman Empire, but he was murdered soon afterward. In 27 BC, his adopted son, Octavian, or Augustus, became the first emperor.

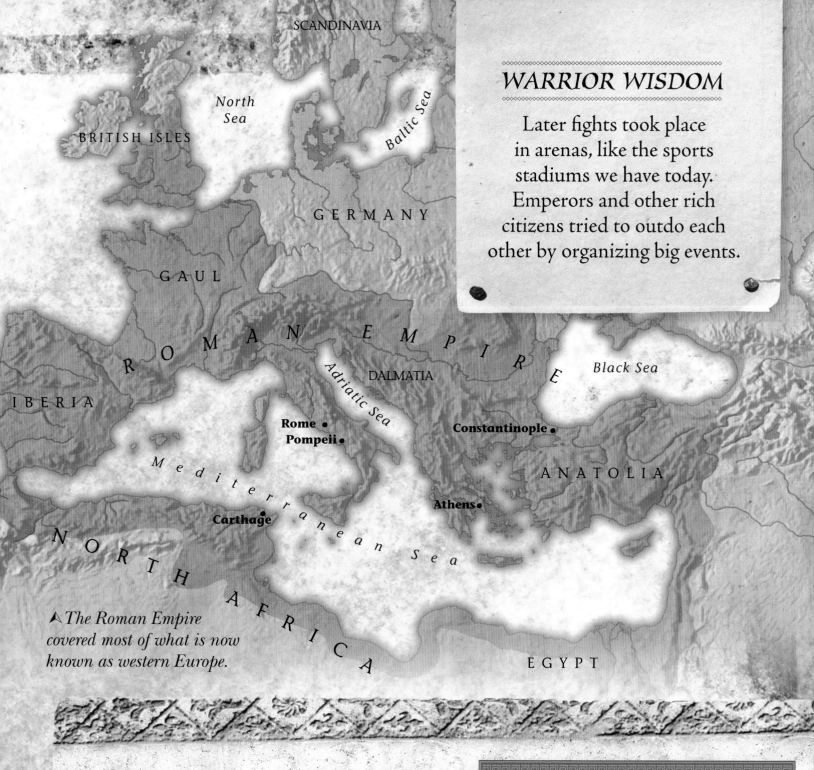

SCANDINAVIA

*North Sea*

BRITISH ISLES

*Baltic Sea*

GERMANY

GAUL

R O M A N   E M P I R E

DALMATIA

*Adriatic Sea*

Black Sea

IBERIA

Rome •
Pompeii •

Constantinople •

A N A T O L I A

*Mediterranean Sea*

Athens •

Carthage •

N O R T H   A F R I C A

EGYPT

➤ *The Roman Empire covered most of what is now known as western Europe.*

# THE FIRST FIGHTERS

The Romans weren't the only ancient people to enjoy bloody fights. In fact, they may have gotten the idea from the Etruscans or the Campanians—two peoples in Italy who enjoyed watching men fight.

# GLADIATOR SCHOOL

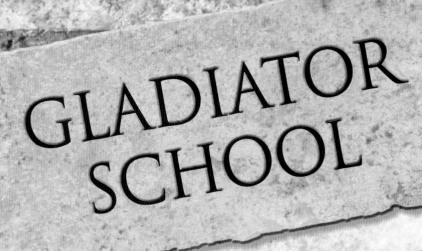

Gladiators needed to put on a good show for the audience. They had to go to a special school, called a *ludus*. Many of the teachers had been successful gladiators themselves.

## Ludus

When a man joined a *ludus* at the age of about 17, he swore an oath, or promise. In this oath he agreed to being burned, chained, and beaten by his teachers when training, and to being killed in the ring. Most gladiators lived at the school and were guarded so that they could not escape.

## Training

Gladiators trained using wooden weapons. They practiced by attacking a wooden post stuck in the ground, or sometimes a sack filled with straw. Gladiators lived together and trained together in the *ludus*. Many of them became friends.

◁ *The* ludus *had a small arena where gladiators practised their fighting skills.*

## GLADIATOR

The film *Gladiator* (2000) is about a fictional general named Maximus Decimus Meridius. He refuses to serve the emperor's son, who has killed his own father to control the empire. Maximus is sold into a *ludus*.

# RETIARII, MYRMILLONES, AND SAMNES

**D**ifferent types of gladiator used various kinds of weapons and armor. Gladiators such as *retiarii*, *myrmillones*, and *samnes* didn't wear much armor at all.

## Retiarii

The name *retiarii* means "net men" in Latin. These gladiators fought with a net and a **spear** with three tips, called a **trident**. They only wore armor on their left arm and shoulder and tried to capture their enemy in the net before they attacked them.

### WARRIOR WISDOM

*Retiarii* were trained to fight gladiators called *secutores* ("chasers"). These gladiators wore helmets with very small eye holes to stop *retiarii* stabbing them in the face with their tridents.

▲Retiarii *tried to capture their enemy by throwing a net over them.*

## Myrmillones

These gladiators wore helmets with a large, finlike **crest**. They carried a sword and a large shield. *Myrmillones'* arms and legs were wrapped in fabric. *Myrmillones* never fought each other.

▲ *The crests of myrmillones' helmets were made of horse hair.*

## Samnes

*Samnes* gladiators were named after a group of tribes who fought many battles against Rome. They wore a helmet, armor on their sword arm, and a **greave** on one leg.

➤ Samnes *carried a short sword and rectangular shield.*

# PROVOCATORES, EQUITES, AND VELITES

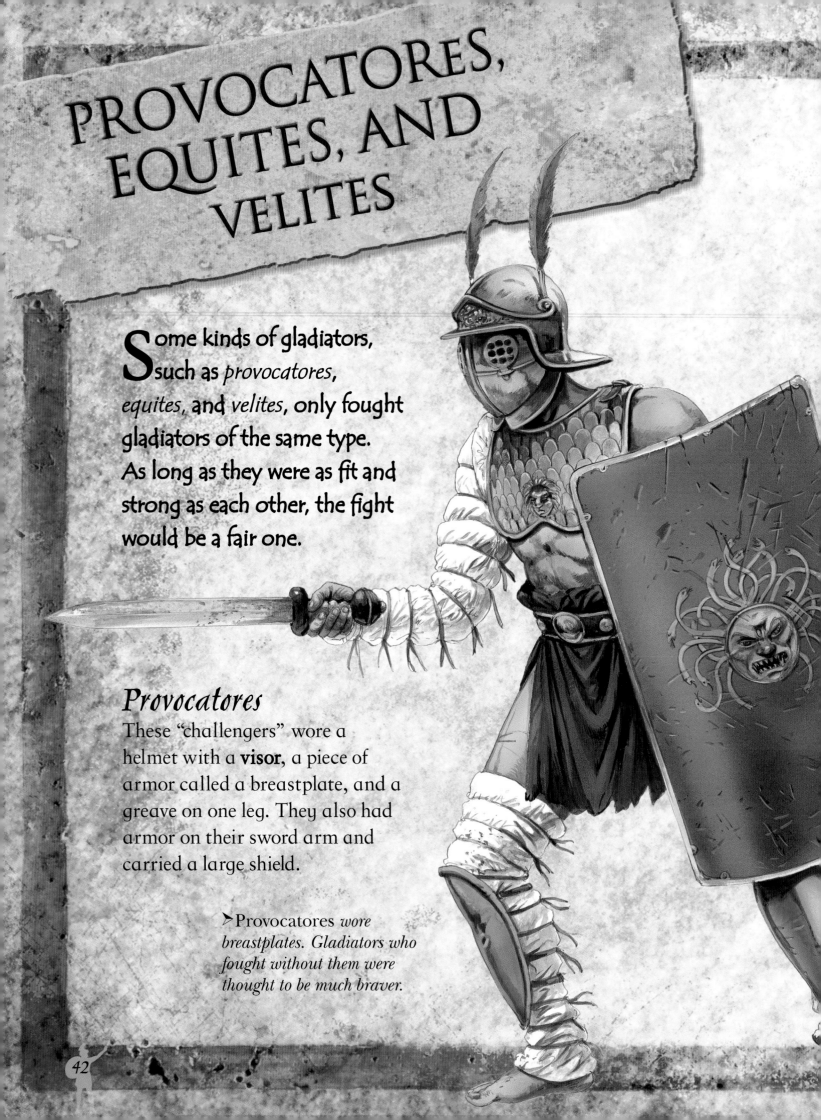

S ome kinds of gladiators, such as *provocatores*, *equites*, and *velites*, only fought gladiators of the same type. As long as they were as fit and strong as each other, the fight would be a fair one.

## Provocatores

These "challengers" wore a helmet with a **visor**, a piece of armor called a breastplate, and a greave on one leg. They also had armor on their sword arm and carried a large shield.

➤ *Provocatores wore breastplates. Gladiators who fought without them were thought to be much braver.*

## Equites

These gladiators fought on horseback. Their name, *equites*, means "horsemen" in Latin. *Equites* wore a helmet and a tunic and wrapped their legs and sword arm in fabric. They also carried a round shield. *Equites* only fought other *equites*.

## Velites

*Velites* had a special spear that was attached to a long strap. It could be pulled back so the gladiator could throw the spear again and again. The Latin name for this kind of spear was *hasta amentata*. *Amentare* meant "to throw something using a strap."

◄ *Some soldiers were called* velites *in the Roman army. These gladiators were named after them.*

◄ Equites *used a long lance and a sword in a fight.*

### WARRIOR WISDOM

Gladiators were fed plenty of food, including beans and barley, so that they had the energy to train and become strong. For this reason, they were often referred to as *hordearii*, or "barley men."

# GLADIATORS OF THE EMPIRE

*◄ The griffin on thraeces' helmets had an eagle's head and a lion's body.*

**M**any emperors used the games as a way of showing how powerful they were in comparison to tribes they had conquered. They also helped the tribes feel they were part of the empire, protected by the strength of Rome. As the empire grew, gladiator fighting spread far and wide.

## Thraeces

These gladiators (named after the Thracian tribe) wore protection on their sword arms. **Thraeces** had small, rectangular shields and used curved swords. Their helmets were decorated with a griffin—a creature that the Romans believed guarded the dead.

## Hoplomachi

The armor of **hoplomachi** was similar to *thraeces*' armor. Unlike the *thraeces*, *hoplomachi* used a rectangular shield and fought with a spear and sword. They threw the spear at their enemy early on in the fight and then fought the rest of the battle with the sword. *Hoplomachi* looked like one of Rome's old enemies, the Greek hoplite soldiers. This is where the name *hoplomachi* comes from.

◄Hoplomachi *had very similar helmets to* thraeces.

## EMPERORS IN THE RING

Some emperors even fought as gladiators themselves. Emperor Commodus (AD 180–192) claimed to have fought hundreds of times without getting hurt—no one dared harm the emperor!

# THE COLOSSEUM

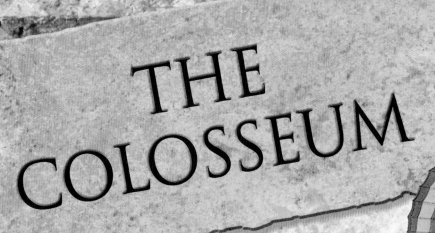

In AD 80, a new amphitheater was opened to the public in Rome. It was a large, circular building with seats around the outside and a large space in the middle for entertainment. It was later to be known as the Colosseum.

**Seating**

## Let the games begin

The Colosseum was meant to please the public. To celebrate its opening, gladiator games went on for 100 days. The Colosseum could seat up to 50,000 people and towered over the city of Rome, at more than 187 feet (57 meters) in height.

**Corridor**

*◄ The audience in the Colosseum watched the games from many tiers, or levels, of seating.*

**Awning**

**Arena**

## Sea battles

Many people believe that Emperor Titus had the Colosseum's arena flooded with water, so that a "sea" battle could be staged, with gladiators fighting on board ships.

*▲ If a sea battle, or naumachia, took place at the Colosseum, it would have been small. Larger battles were staged outside Rome in river basins.*

# THE BUILD-UP

Most gladiator games were held on public holidays. Advertisements for the games, with lists of the fighters, were painted on the city walls. Some people bet money on which gladiator they thought would win.

## On parade

Gladiators were owned by rich men. Many of these men brought them to town especially for the games. They walked through the streets while someone called out their names and skills. This was so people could decide who they thought was a winner.

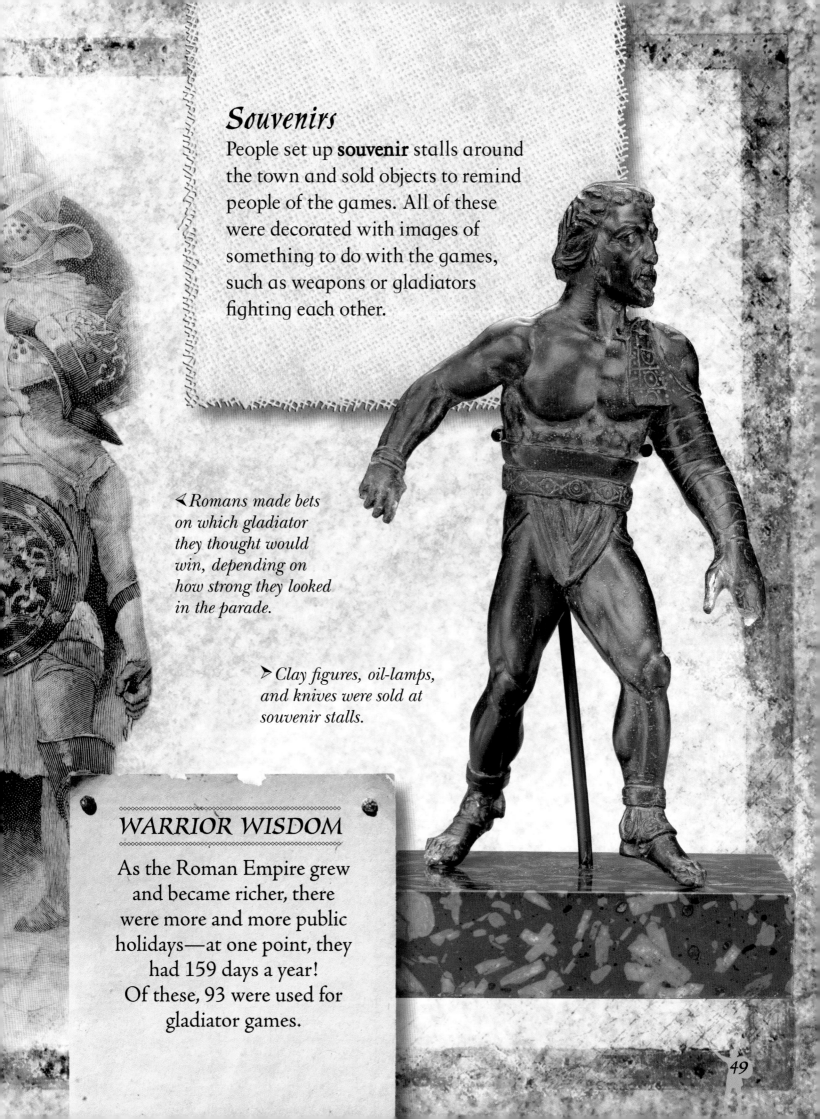

## Souvenirs

People set up **souvenir** stalls around the town and sold objects to remind people of the games. All of these were decorated with images of something to do with the games, such as weapons or gladiators fighting each other.

◄ *Romans made bets on which gladiator they thought would win, depending on how strong they looked in the parade.*

► *Clay figures, oil-lamps, and knives were sold at souvenir stalls.*

### WARRIOR WISDOM

As the Roman Empire grew and became richer, there were more and more public holidays—at one point, they had 159 days a year! Of these, 93 were used for gladiator games.

# THE AUDIENCE

▼ The audience watches as gladiators salute the emperor Julius Caesar before the fights begin.

Tickets for the games were given to people of the highest classes and passed on to friends and supporters. They then passed them on to their friends, and so on, down to the lower classes.

## The best seats in the house

Depending on their place in society, different people were allowed into different areas of the Colosseum. Closest to the ring were the very rich and important men. The emperor, of course, had the best seat in the house—right at the front.

## The general public

Women and girls sat in the highest seats, furthest from the stage. These were the worst seats in the house for watching the action. Below the women were slaves and poor people, then soldiers and ordinary citizens.

## RIOT!

Public games were very noisy and busy. A fresco, or wall painting, at Pompeii shows a riot in the crowd that took place in AD 59. Many people were killed or wounded. Gladiator shows were banned in Pompeii for years afterward.

# THE BIG DAY

There were many different kinds of events to entertain the audience on the day of the games. The show usually started with animal hunts and criminal executions. It was not until the afternoon that the gladiators began to fight.

## Animal hunts

In the morning, creatures such as bulls and elephants were released into the ring to fight each other. Sometimes they were hunted by men armed with spears. Exotic animals from around the empire were shown to the audience to remind them how much of the world was ruled by the Romans.

*Sometimes the animals were so scared that they had to be chased by other men to make them fight the gladiators.*

## WARRIOR WISDOM

Emperor Augustus (63 BC–AD 19) boasted that in the 26 wild animal hunts he put on, 3,500 creatures were killed. In the opening games at the Colosseum, Emperor Titus (AD 39–91) had 9,000 animals killed.

## The warm-up

The afternoon's entertainment often began with comedy fights. Next, there was a parade of men carrying the weapons and armor for the gladiators. The gladiators then had a warm-up fight. When the trumpets sounded, it was time for the gladiators to get ready for the main event.

# FIGHT!

Gladiators normally fought one-to-one. The two men were equally matched in strength so the fight would not end too quickly.

◁ *Each gladiator was fighting for his life. If he fought well, he might be spared.*

## Showdown

A typical afternoon at the gladiator games involved around ten to 12 fights. Fights might be anything from two to 15 minutes long. Some fights lasted so long that both gladiators were too exhausted to go on. In these cases, they were allowed to live.

# Spartacus

Spartacus was a gladiator who led a revolt against the Romans in 73 BC. He escaped from his *ludus* with other men, but they were defeated in 71 BC by the Roman army. Stanley Kubrick made a film in 1960 about the life of Spartacus, starring Kirk Douglas.

## Going back in time

Sometimes gladiators were made to **re-enact** famous battles. In 46 BC, Julius Caesar ordered a huge battle. Each army had 500 foot soldiers, 20 elephants, and 30 gladiators on horseback.

▼ *Re-enactments of famous battles could involve many gladiators at a time.*

# WIN OR LOSE

Gladiators usually fought until it was clear that one of them was going to win. A gladiator always tried to impress the audience with his skill so that, even if he lost, the audience might encourage the emperor to let him live.

## Decision time

If the emperor decided that the loser should die, the winning gladiator had to cut the loser's throat. The winner tried to make the death a quick one. The loser might have been a friend from his *ludus*.

➤ *The winning gladiator looked to the emperor to see whether he should kill his opponent or let him live.*

## Thumbs up or thumbs down

It was the right of the emperor, or the person who had paid for the games, to decide whether a loser would live or die. The public used their thumbs to show whether they wanted the loser to live or not—but it is not known which way the audience held their thumbs when they did this.

### WARRIOR WISDOM

If a gladiator died in the fight, the audience wanted to make sure that he was dead. The gladiator was poked with a hot iron to see if he reacted. After he had been taken out of the ring, his throat would be cut, just to be on the safe side!

# THE END OF GLADIATORS

By the AD 400s, the Roman Empire had become weaker. It was attacked by many enemies, and its leaders often fought for power among themselves.

## End of the show

Emperor Constantine banned the games in AD 326. Other emperors tried to start them up again, but they never became as popular as they once had been. In AD 400, Emperor Honorius banned them forever.

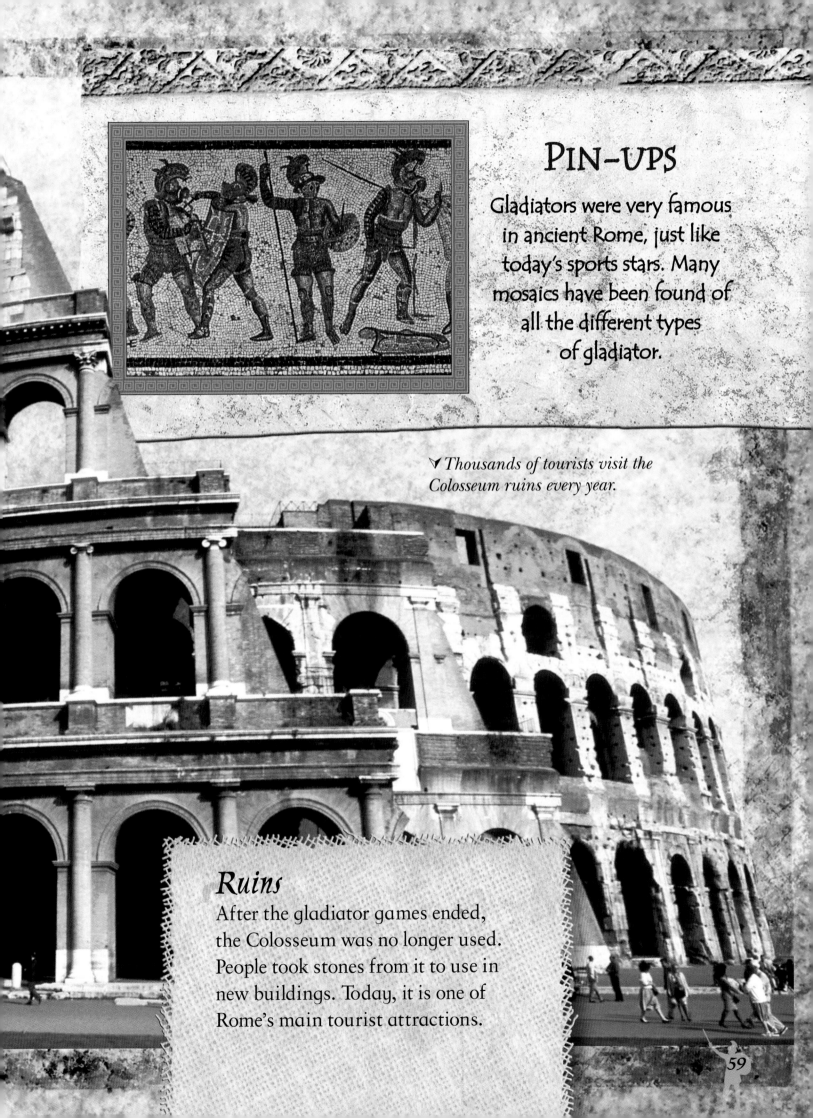

# PIN-UPS

Gladiators were very famous in ancient Rome, just like today's sports stars. Many mosaics have been found of all the different types of gladiator.

▼ *Thousands of tourists visit the Colosseum ruins every year.*

## Ruins

After the gladiator games ended, the Colosseum was no longer used. People took stones from it to use in new buildings. Today, it is one of Rome's main tourist attractions.

# CONTENTS

# WHAT WAS A SAMURAI?

Samurai were Japanese warriors. They were known for being fierce and brave. Between 1000 and 1800 in Japan, samurai were very powerful members of **clans**, or groups of related families.

## The way of the warrior

Samurai warriors followed a special code, called **Bushido**, or "The Way of the Warrior." The code said that samurai must be honorable and loyal to their master. A samurai was expected to fight bravely and be happy to give up his life for his lord.

➤ *In **battle**, samurai wore full **armor** and carried their **nobori**, or family banner.*

## The First Emperor

In Japanese myth, the Sun goddess Amaterasu sent her grandson from Heaven to Earth to be the first **emperor** of Japan.

## Family pride

Samurai were very proud of their family history. Many came from families that had been warriors for several generations, though others were only just learning Bushido. A samurai told stories of his family's bravery to the warrior he was about to fight. He also had his family's history written on a banner, which he carried to war.

▷ Samurai sometimes carried fans called "tessen." They had iron spikes and could be used as weapons.

# WHEN DID SAMURAI LIVE?

Samurai were powerful in Japan from about 1000 to the late 1800s. Early samurai were warriors on horseback. From the early 1600s, samurai were important in government, so they spent less time fighting. They also studied art and **literature**.

## Social classes

Japan had a feudal system. People were in classes, or groups, depending on their importantance. Everyone was loyal to the emperor, but the **Bushi**, or samurai class, were in charge of running the country, so they ruled the lower classes.

▽ *For a samurai on horseback, the most important weapon was a a bow.*

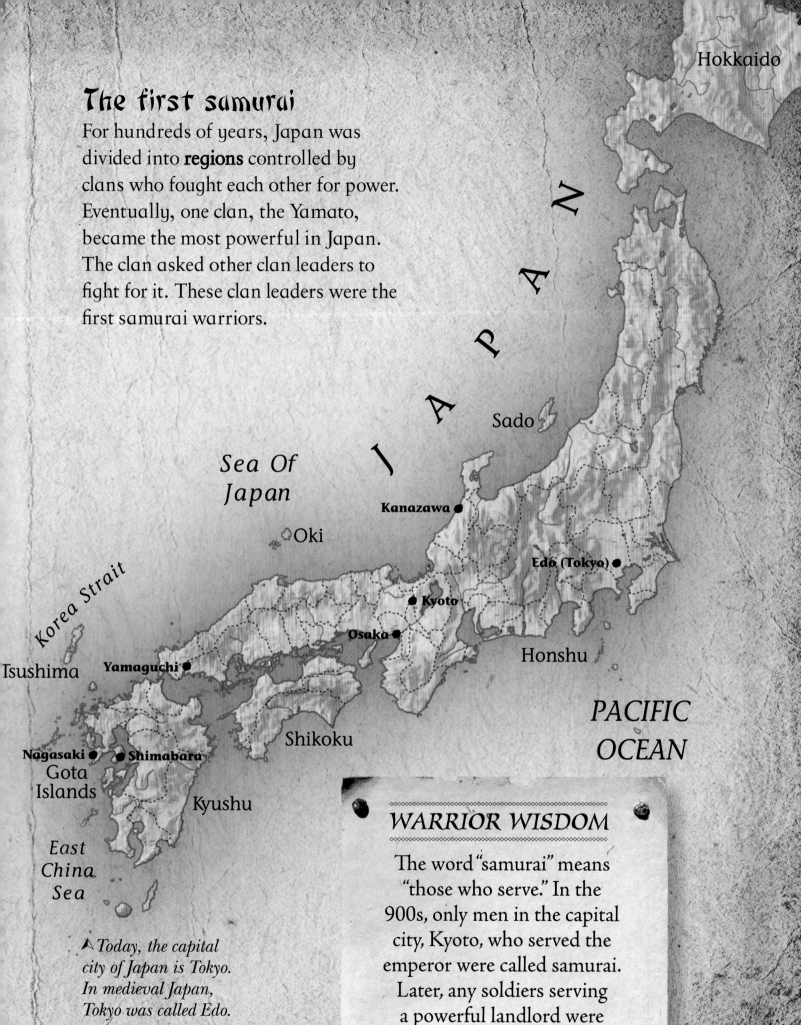

## The first samurai

For hundreds of years, Japan was divided into **regions** controlled by clans who fought each other for power. Eventually, one clan, the Yamato, became the most powerful in Japan. The clan asked other clan leaders to fight for it. These clan leaders were the first samurai warriors.

Hokkaido

JAPAN

Sado

Sea Of Japan

Kanazawa

Oki

Edo (Tokyo)

Kyoto

Osaka

Honshu

Korea Strait

Tsushima

Yamaguchi

PACIFIC OCEAN

Shikoku

Nagasaki  Shimabara

Gota Islands

Kyushu

East China Sea

Today, the capital city of Japan is Tokyo. In medieval Japan, Tokyo was called Edo.

### WARRIOR WISDOM

The word "samurai" means "those who serve." In the 900s, only men in the capital city, Kyoto, who served the emperor were called samurai. Later, any soldiers serving a powerful landlord were called samurai.

65

# BECOMING A SAMURAI

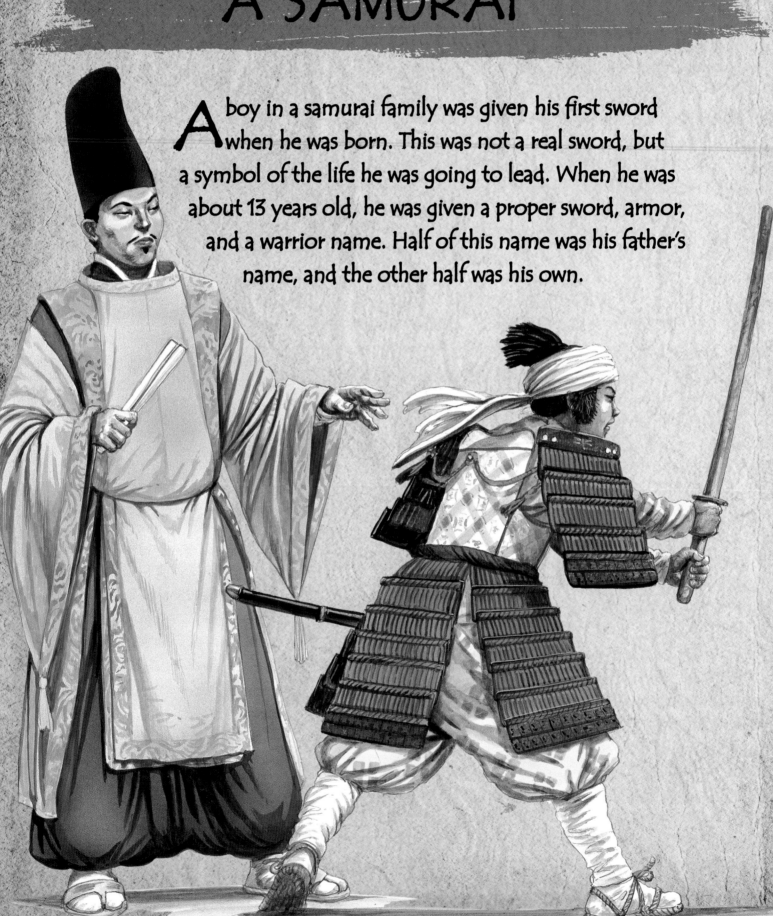

A boy in a samurai family was given his first sword when he was born. This was not a real sword, but a symbol of the life he was going to lead. When he was about 13 years old, he was given a proper sword, armor, and a warrior name. Half of this name was his father's name, and the other half was his own.

## Stages of training

Samurai boys were brought up not to fear death or danger. They began training at three years old with their father, using wooden swords. They were given real weapons at 13 years old and sent to a relative or **fencing** teacher. They were in training until they were 20 years old.

▽ *It was important for samurai boys to practice their sword skills.*

## Warrior woman

Tomoe Gozen (*c.*1157–1247) was a female samurai. She fought alongside her husband, Minamoto no Yoshinaka, and was a great swordswoman and **archer**.

## Girls and women

The wives and daughters of samurai were expected to look after the home. Girls learned to handle money and run the household. Female samurai warriors, such as Tomoe Gozen, were rare.

# THE PEN AND THE SWORD

櫻ノ詩　兒島髙德

Samurai were expected to be able to read and write as well as they could fight. Warriors who could do both well were admired. When they were not fighting, samurai studied culture and the arts.

## Inspirational art

Samurai were often the subject of paintings. Images of heroes or imaginary great warriors helped samurai to remember the bravery of others and to follow Bushido.

> ➤ The samurai Kojima no Takanori writes a poem on a cherry tree.

## Fighting talk

The Heike Monogatari, or Tale of the Heike, is a collection of stories about two clans, the Taira and Minamoto. Samurai studied these stories because the heroes of the stories were seen as good examples for samurai to follow.

➤ *The battles between the Taira and Minamoto clans were known as the Gempei War.*

## Taira no Tadamori

Taira no Tadamori (1096-1153) was a very important samurai, famous for both his writing and fighting skills. He was said to have been the first warrior to serve the emperor at court.

# WEAPONS

**S**amurai had many different weapons. When they were on horseback, samurai fought with a bow, so they could fire arrows at the enemy from far away. They also carried a long and a short sword, and sometimes a dagger and spear.

▲ *Samurai on horseback used a bow and arrows when charging into battle.*

## Long sword

The **katana** was a long, curved sword. It had a single-edged blade and a long handle so it could be held with two hands for extra power. Bushido said that the katana was like the warrior's soul. Samurai often gave their katana a name.

➤ *Samurai who fought on foot used their katana swords.*

70

*◄ These arrows were used by samurai in the 1300s.*

## Short sword

The **wakizashi** sword was shorter than the katana sword. Together, these two swords were called the **daisho**, which means "big and small."

*▷ Samurai kept the wakizashi sword with them at all times—they even slept with it!*

*▷ A tsuba, or hand guard, stopped the samurai's hand from slipping onto the sword's blade.*

## Bow and arrows

A bow and arrows were the most useful weapons a samurai on horseback could have. Bows were about 8 feet (2.5 meters) long and made of silk and bamboo. Arrows had sharp spikes at the end.

## WARRIOR WISDOM

In 1867, samurai were banned from carrying swords. However, many samurai started to carry their swords secretly. They even hid them in walking sticks!

# ARMOR

The style of armor worn by samurai warriors changed over the centuries. However, the various pieces of samurai armor were always more or less the same.

## Body armor

On the top half of their body, samurai wore a helmet, shoulder guards, chest armor, and one or two arm guards. Their thighs were protected by an apron, or skirt, made of armor. The bottom of their legs was covered by armor that looked like shin pads. They also wore animal skin boots with splints made of brass to protect the feet.

> A suit of samurai armor from the 1500s or 1600s.

Helmet

Shoulder guard

Chest armor

Arm guard

Apron

Animal skin boot

# Helmets

Samurai helmets were designed not only for protection but also to give the warrior a frightening appearance. Sometimes samurai wore a metal face **mask**, which must have made them look terrifying.

◄ *A helmet decorated with a war fan. Samurai used fans for signaling and sending commands.*

▲ *Decorations on top of helmets made it easy to recognize samurai on the battlefield.*

# The Red Devils

The samurai Li Naomasa had the armor of all his troops colored red. This made it easy to recognize each other, and also scared the enemy. Soon they were known as "The Red Devils."

# NINJA

According to Bushido, samurai could not carry out secret tasks. From the 1300s to the 1600s, this work was carried out by ninja. Ninja were free to carry out any orders.

## The art of the ninja

**Ninjutsu**, the art of the ninja warrior, may have been started by Chinese warriors. They went to Japan for safety when their kingdoms were under attack in the 900s. As part of their training, ninja warriors learned the art of stealth and working undercover.

## Ninja in films

Japanese ninja have appeared in many feature films, including *Teenage Mutant Ninja Turtles* and James Bond films. In *You Only Live Twice* (1967), James trains at a ninja camp in Japan.

## Now you see them, now you don't

Ninja were so good at hiding and surprising an enemy that some people believed that they could become invisible, or turn themselves into animals. A ninja often wore a **shoku** on each hand. This was an iron band that went around the hand, with spikes on the inside.

◄ *People believed that ninja had special powers because they were so good at hiding from enemies.*

▲ *Shoku helped ninja block swords and climb trees like a cat.*

# EARLY CLANS

By the 1000s, there were two very powerful family groupings in Japan. They were the Taira and the Minamoto clans. These families fought each other in the Gempei War.

## Taira strength

After beating the Minamoto clan in 1160, Taira no Kiyomori became the first warrior to be given the job of advisor to the emperor. He eventually took control of the **government** for himself. His clan ruled through the emperor, rather than by themselves.

# Minamoto no Yoritomo

In 1192, Minamoto no Yoritomo took the title of **shogun**. A shogun was a samurai military leader. Yorimoto decided that a samurai could only become a shogun if his father had been one before him.

◄ *The warrior **monk**, Benkei, led the Minamoto clan to battle in the Gempei War.*

# Gempei War

In the Heiji Rebellion of 1160, the Taira beat the Minamoto clan in battle. Their victory did not last long. In 1180, the Minamoto returned and beat the Taira clan. This was the first battle of the Gempei War.

# THE RISE OF THE SAMURAI

After 1100, the samurai clans became more powerful. They got involved in the **politics** of the emperor's court and ruled as shoguns, with the emperor as leader.

## Foot soldiers

After about 1500, Japanese armies had large numbers of foot soldiers. There could be thousands of people fighting in a war, and the shogun, with the help of the samurai commanders, controlled them.

◁ *Minamoto no Yoritomo, shown on horseback, was the first shogun ruler of Japan.*

# Ruling classes

The samurai had a lot of power in Japan. They had a great deal of control over the lives of people from the lower classes. After about 1500, a law made it illegal for anyone except samurai to carry weapons. This stopped the lower classes from rebelling against them.

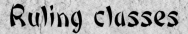

*▼ Samurai were powerful and well respected by the lower classes in Japan.*

## WARRIOR WISDOM

In the late 1000s, the samurai Kamakura Kagemasa was shot in the right eye by an arrow. To remove the arrow, a friend needed to put his foot on Kagemasa's face. This would have been a great dishonor, so he refused.

79

# SAMURAI IN BATTLE

In battle, samurai often fought on horseback as well as on foot. Samurai attacked in groups led by one man. They followed the unit's nobori, or banner.

## Charge!

Samurai on horseback were terrifying. When a battle was going well, a samurai army might break into a charge, chasing the enemy off the battlefield.

> *Samurai always carried the nobori into battle.*

# The Last Samurai

The 2003 film *The Last Samurai*, starring Tom Cruise, is about a soldier who visits Japan after the emperor returns to rule.
He meets a rebel group of samurai warriors and lives among them to learn samurai ways.

▲ One-to-one fights are called **duels**. These fights were usually to settle an argument.

## Revenge

Samurai sometimes challenged each other to a fight, especially if one of the samurai wanted to take revenge against the other. He might want to fight the son of a warrior who had killed his own father.

# THREE GREAT MEN

**B**etween 1400 and 1600, different states of Japan were at war with each other. This was called the Warring States Period. Three samurai leaders managed to make the country one again. They called themselves **daimyo**, or "great names."

## Oda Nobunaga (1534-1582)
One of the most powerful daimyo was Oda Nobunaga. He defeated the rulers of Kyoto and took over the city in 1568. Hideyoshi and Ieyasu were his followers.

### WARRIOR WISDOM

The family of shoguns called the Tokugawa made sure the other daimyo stayed loyal by putting them in charge of their own lands. The daimyo lived in their castle towns, but their families lived in Edo, the capital city. Each daimyo only met his family once a year when he marched to Edo to pay respect to the shogun.

*⋀Oda Nobunaga tried to unite Japan under one ruler, but he died before he could succeed.*

# Toyotomi Hideyoshi (1536-1598)

Toyotomi Hideyoshi was one of Oda Nobunaga's most trusted men. When he heard that Nobunaga had been killed, Hideyoshi began to take control. By 1591, he ruled a large part of Japan. As he was not from the Minamoto family, he could not call himself a shogun. However, when he died, his five-year-old son became ruler.

➤ *Hideyoshi blows on a conch shell trumpet to signal to his people.*

# Tokugawa Ieyasu (1542-1616)

After the death of Hideyoshi, some people were happy with his son as ruler, but others were not. These people supported Tokugawa Ieyasu. The two sides fought at Sekigahara in 1600, and Ieyasu won. As he was from the Minamoto family, he named himself shogun.

◄ *Tokugawa Ieyasu was named shogun in 1603. From then on, Tokugawa shoguns ruled Japan until the mid-1800s.*

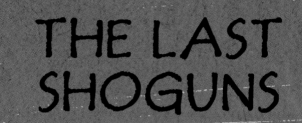

# THE LAST SHOGUNS

In 1639, the shogun banned trade with European countries. Japan only began to trade with Europe again in the 1800s. Many samurai did not like this and wanted to remove the Tokugawa shogun who allowed it. They succeeded, and in 1868, Emperor Meiji became Japan's new ruler.

◄ *Tokugawa Yoshinobu was Japan's last shogun.*

## Emperor Meiji's army

Almost as soon as Meiji took control, he stripped the shoguns of all their power. Meiji also thought that a modern army, such as the armies of Europe, would be better than the samurai system. He even encouraged foreign trade. This annoyed the samurai who had made him ruler.

➤ *Emperor Meiji was also known as Mutsuhito.*

## Western samurai

Few men from the west were allowed to be samurai, but at least two western sailors were made samurai by Shogun Tokugawa. One was the English adventurer William Adams (1564–1620). He was given the daisho swords and called Miura Anjin.

## Kumamoto Castle

The daimyo of Satsuma had a strong army, armed with both samurai swords and guns. They decided to challenge Emperor Meiji. In 1877, they attacked one of the emperor's most important castles, Kumamoto. After a long battle, Emperor Meiji's army beat the samurai.

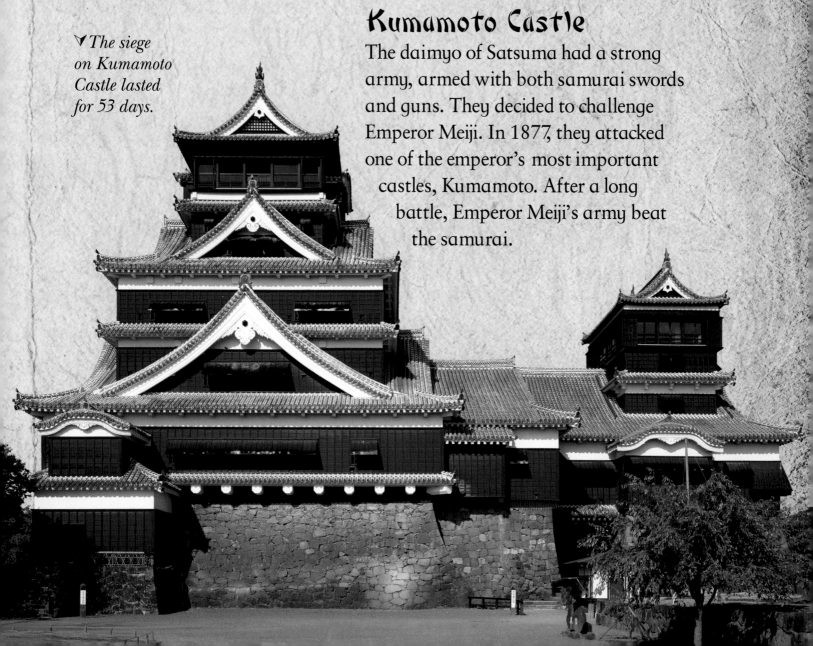

*⌄ The siege on Kumamoto Castle lasted for 53 days.*

# THE DECLINE OF SAMURAI

Samurai became less powerful after the 1600s because guns began to be used in Japan. The defeat of the Satsuma Rebellion made them lose even more faith in their strength. Although samurai clans still existed, they never regained the power they once had.

## Osaka Castle

Osaka Castle was the home of the Toyotomi clan. Tokugawa Ieyasu had been shogun since 1603, but in 1614 he still feared the Toyotomi clan, so he attacked Osaka Castle. For days, Ieyasu fired cannons at the walls and, eventually, Hideyori Toyotomi signed a peace **treaty**, or agreement. Soon after, the fighting began again. Osaka Castle was finally taken over in June 1615, and the Tokugawa clan continued to rule Japan for more than two centuries. Today, the castle has been rebuilt. It is seen as a symbol of the great power and bravery of the samurai.

▲ *Osaka Castle was built high up on stone to protect it from attackers.*

## A good example

Samurai are still looked up to as examples of good behavior. Great warriors are role models for the Japanese people to follow, and the Bushido code is still seen as a good way of life. There are many films, books, and **monuments** that celebrate the bravery and honor of samurai.

▲*A statue of Kusunoki Masashige in the Imperial Palace Gardens in Tokyo, Japan.*

## Jedi

The Jedi warriors in the *Star Wars* films trained in a similar way to samurai. The character of Darth Vader even wore a costume based on samurai armor.

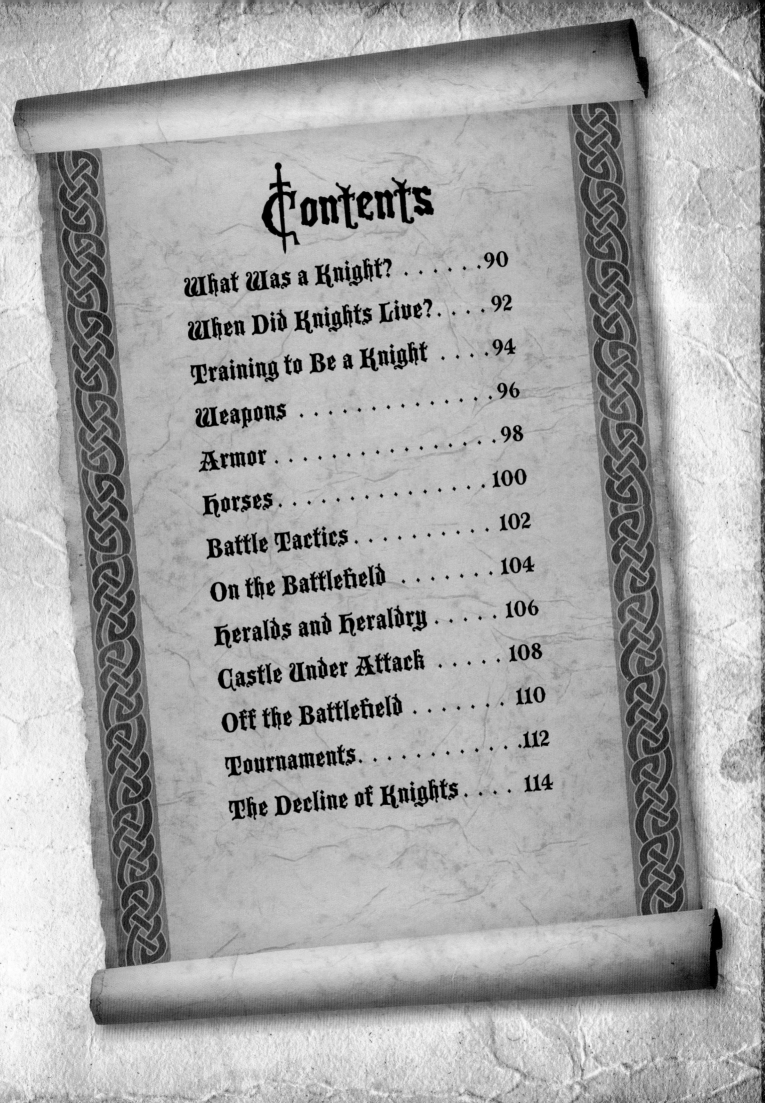

# Contents

# What Was a Knight?

**K**nights were nobles who fought on horseback in the Middle Ages (AD 500–1500). They were the most powerful and feared fighters of their time.

## FIGHTING FAMILIES

The king or other knights decided who could become a knight. If a man's father had been a knight, then it was likely he would be, too. Knights fought when their king or lord needed them in a battle. Knights had to be wealthy because it was expensive to have a horse, armor, and weapons.

➤ *Knights were the most powerful fighting force on the battlefield and were feared by those on foot.*

## CODE OF HONOR

Knights were so powerful that kings sometimes found them difficult to control. Some knights followed the code of **chivalry**. This was a set of rules for good conduct or behavior.

➤ *If a knight surrendered in battle, the knight fighting him was supposed to let him live.*

# The Knights of the Round Table

*Storytellers in the Middle Ages told exciting tales about a legendary king called Arthur and his chivalrous knights. They were said to have sat at a round table, so that none of them seemed more important than any of the others.*

# When Did Knights Live?

**K**nights lived in Europe in the Middle Ages. Kings and nobles fought constantly for land and power. Knights defended their lord or king. They fought in wars and battles at home and in other countries.

## HOLY WAR

Jerusalem, in Israel, was a holy place for Muslims, Christians, and Jews. When Muslim Turks took control of Jerusalem in 1095, the Pope called for European Christians to lead a war of **religion**, or **crusade**, against them.

## WARRIOR WISDOM

Most countries in Europe had a **feudal system**. The king owned the land, but loaned it to barons and earls. Then, they gave land to lesser nobles and provided men as soldiers. The land was worked on by **peasants**.

SCOTLAND

IRELAND

*North Sea*

ENGLAND

WALES

**AGINCOURT** ▲

*Normandy*

ATLANTIC OCEAN

FRANCE

NAVARRE

LEON-CASTILE

ARAGON

CATALONIA

ALMORAVID EMPIRE

⌃ *Knights fought against each other throughout Europe as well as in the Middle East.*

NORWAY

SWEDEN

Baltic Sea

DENMARK

POMERANIA

POLAND

HOLY ROMAN EMPIRE

HUNGARY

PAPAL STATES

•Rome

NORMAN ITALY

BYZANTINE EMPIRE

Antioch•

Rhodes•

Mediterranean Sea

➤ *Peasants who were owned by the lord were called* **serfs**.

## FARMING THE LAND

Most peasants had to work on the lord's land, but there was some land to be shared by villagers as well. Open land was ploughed into long, narrow strips. Peasants had to work hard for very little reward.

# Training to Be a Knight

Training to be a knight took many years. If a noble's son was to become a knight, he was sent at about seven years old to live with another noble to be trained. Boys in training were called pages.

## KNIGHT SCHOOL

Pages learned basic fighting skills, often with wooden swords and shields. They were also taught good manners. At 14 years old, pages became squires. They later accompanied the knight that they served into battle.

➤ *Pages used wooden weapons so they didn't seriously hurt each other.*

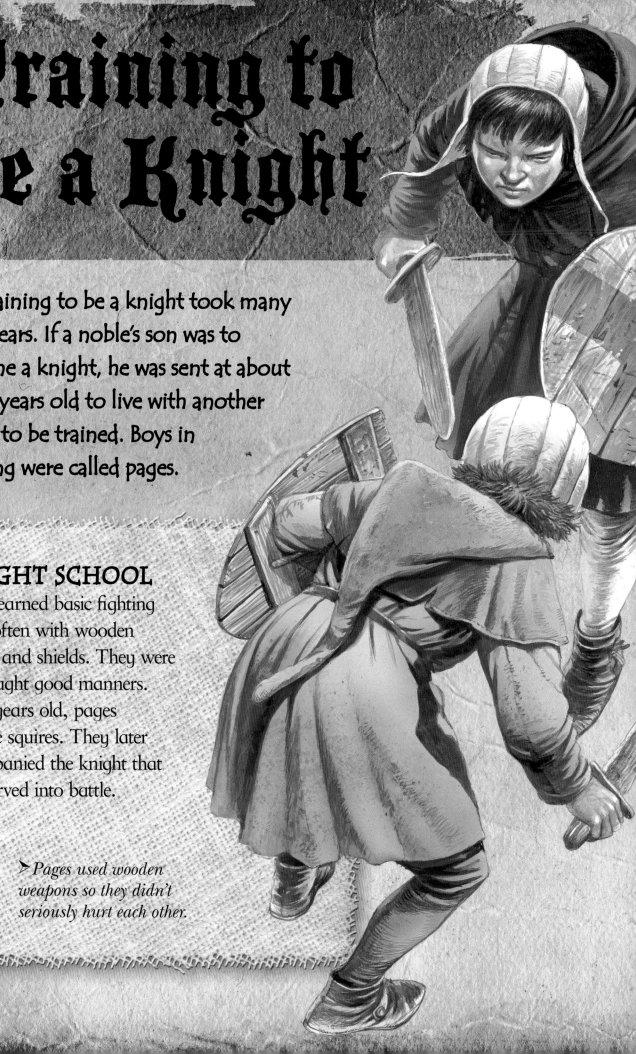

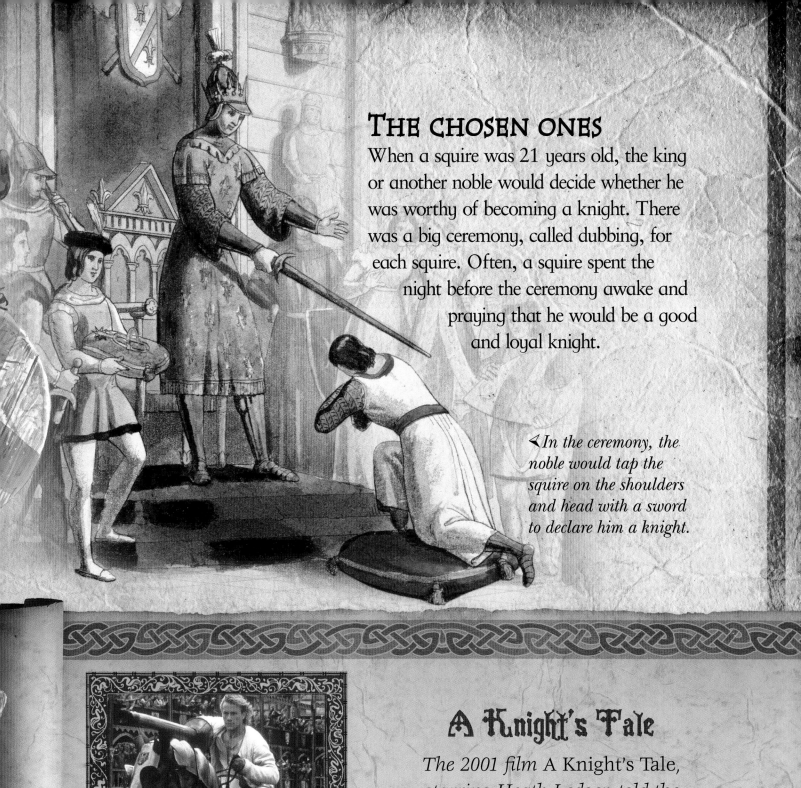

# THE CHOSEN ONES

When a squire was 21 years old, the king or another noble would decide whether he was worthy of becoming a knight. There was a big ceremony, called dubbing, for each squire. Often, a squire spent the night before the ceremony awake and praying that he would be a good and loyal knight.

*◁In the ceremony, the noble would tap the squire on the shoulders and head with a sword to declare him a knight.*

# A Knight's Tale

*The 2001 film A Knight's Tale, starring Heath Ledger, told the story of a young squire who entered **jousting tournaments** after the knight he worked for died. He used a different name so he could pretend to be a knight.*

# Weapons

Knights needed different weapons, depending on whether they were on the ground or on horseback. Each weapon had its uses at different stages of a battle.

Heavy metal head

## MACE

A mace had a metal or wooden handle and a metal head. A good blow from a mace could knock a knight off his horse.

## POLEAX

A poleax was often used by foot soldiers. The ax blade could slice through flesh and even armor.

Blade

## SWORD

A sword was a metal weapon with a sharp blade. It had a crossguard to stop the holder's hands from slipping down the blade.

Crossguard

# Godfrey de Bouillon

*Godfrey de Bouillon led the First Crusade in 1096. This was a battle for an area called the Holy Land in the Middle East. People said he was so strong that he once beheaded a camel with his sword.*

**Handle**

## DAGGER

A dagger was used for stabbing the enemy at close range. In the middle of a battle on the ground, a dagger could be more useful than a sword.

**Sharp edge**

## LANCE

A lance was a long, wooden weapon with a sharp metal point. It was usually carried by knights on horseback. They held out their lances in front of them when they charged at the enemy.

*⊳Knights used lances to knock each other off their horses.*

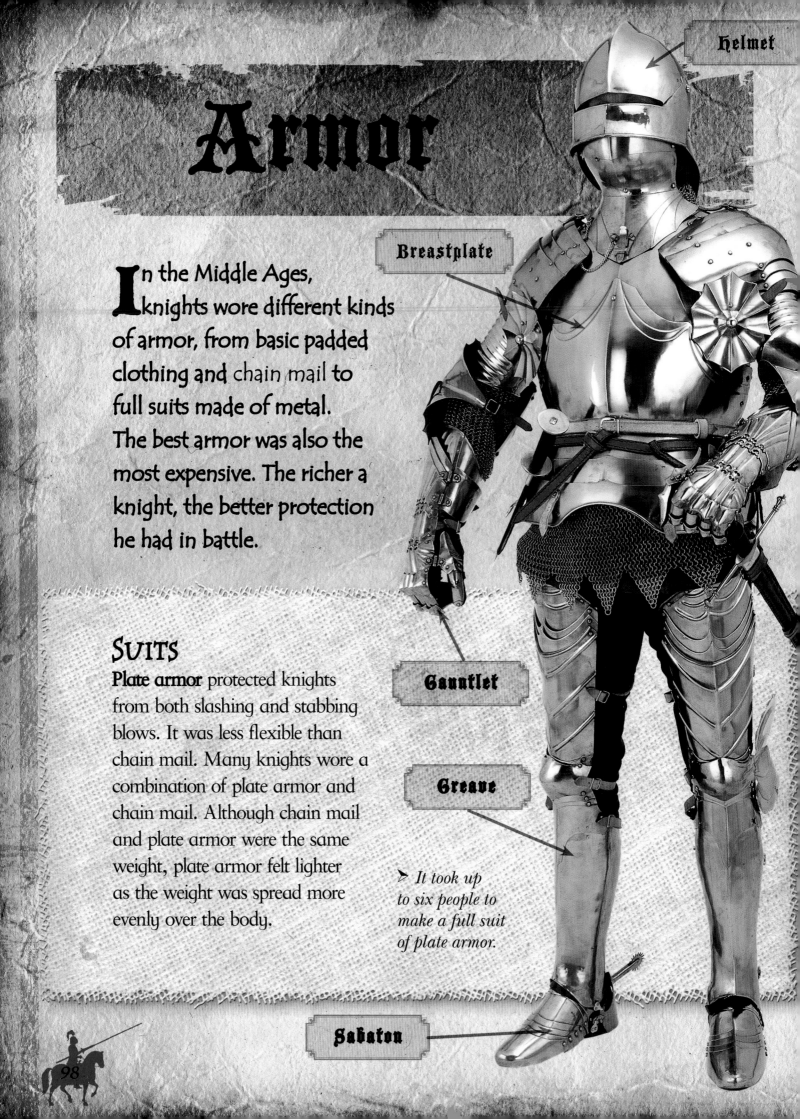

# Armor

In the Middle Ages, knights wore different kinds of armor, from basic padded clothing and chain mail to full suits made of metal. The best armor was also the most expensive. The richer a knight, the better protection he had in battle.

## SUITS

**Plate armor** protected knights from both slashing and stabbing blows. It was less flexible than chain mail. Many knights wore a combination of plate armor and chain mail. Although chain mail and plate armor were the same weight, plate armor felt lighter as the weight was spread more evenly over the body.

➤ It took up to six people to make a full suit of plate armor.

Helmet

Breastplate

Gauntlet

Greave

Sabaton

# Headgear

Helmets were one of the most important parts of a knight's armor. There were many different types of helmets that developed over time, ranging from small, round ones worn with a chain-mail hood, to full plate armor helmets with a **visor**.

➤ *Early helmets were mostly shaped like a cap with chain mail attached. Later, helmets covered more of the face.*

Chain mail

Visor

# Linking rings

Chain mail was made of lots of tiny metal rings linked together. It was very flexible, and it protected the wearer from being slashed by a sword. However, the rings could be forced apart by a stabbing blow. Chain mail rusted easily and was difficult to clean.

◁ *Chain mail could be made into a hood, tunic, or even pants.*

# Shields

A knight used his shield to protect his legs as well as his body. He carried his shield on the opposite side to his fighting arm.

➤ *The lion on the shield is "rampant" on its back legs.*

# Horses

**R**ich knights often had more than one horse. Many had one for traveling and another for carrying his belongings. Heavier, stronger horses were used on the battlefield. A knight's horses were probably his most valued possessions.

> *A horse had to be strong to carry the weight of its own armor, as well as a knight's.*

## HORSE ARMOR

A horse's armor was very important. The richer the knight, the better his horse's protection would be. The most basic armor was a piece of padded cloth called a caparison, which covered the horse's whole body. Some horses even wore plate armor.

*^ Caparisons sometimes had a symbol, or **coat-of-arms**, to help identify the knight.*

## Saddle

The high back of a saddle was called a cantel. The pommel, or high front, protected the knight's stomach and stopped him from being thrown over his horse's head.

## Shaffron

The shaffron protected the front of the horse's head and ears. Some shaffrons had raised areas around the eyeholes so the horse could not see straight ahead. This stopped the horse from being startled, or scared, in battle.

## Peytral

The most important part of the horse to protect was the chest. Chest armor was called a peytral. Not all knights could afford armor for their horses as well as themselves. If a knight's horse was hurt, it would put him in danger.

## Stirrup

The knight placed his feet in stirrups. This helped the knight stay in the saddle when he was hit by another knight's lance.

## Horseshoe

If a horse has to walk on wet ground for a long time, its hooves become soft and its feet sore. The knight's horse had a piece of metal called a horseshoe nailed onto each hoof to protect it. Horseshoes are still used today.

# Battle Tactics

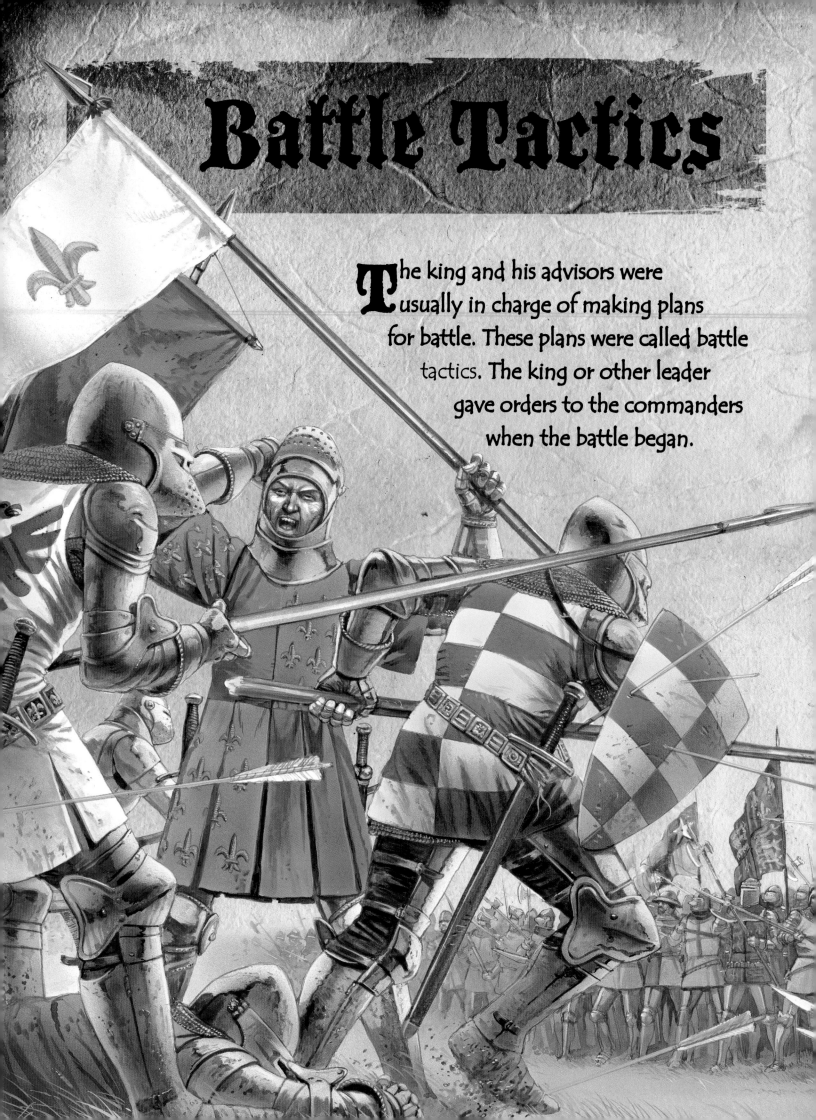

The king and his advisors were usually in charge of making plans for battle. These plans were called battle tactics. The king or other leader gave orders to the commanders when the battle began.

# Richard the Lionheart

*King Richard I of England (1157–1199) was given the nickname "Lionheart" because of his bravery in battle. At 16 years old, he led his army to victory against his father's enemies in France.*

## IN COMMAND

Before the battle started, the king told the commanders what the tactics were. Once fighting began, it was not easy to change the plan. The commanders were far away from each other, so it was difficult to speak to all of them at once. Horns and flags signaled the start of the fight and showed **troops** where to go on the field.

*The troops at the front of the French army, the vanguard, carried banners as they moved toward the English during the famous Battle of Agincourt (1415).*

## BATTLE FORMATION

Commanders had to make plans about where the groups of soldiers and knights would be positioned within the whole army. This was called a battle formation. Some soldiers used weapons called pikes. These soldiers were often placed at the front of the army to frighten the enemy's **cavalry** horses.

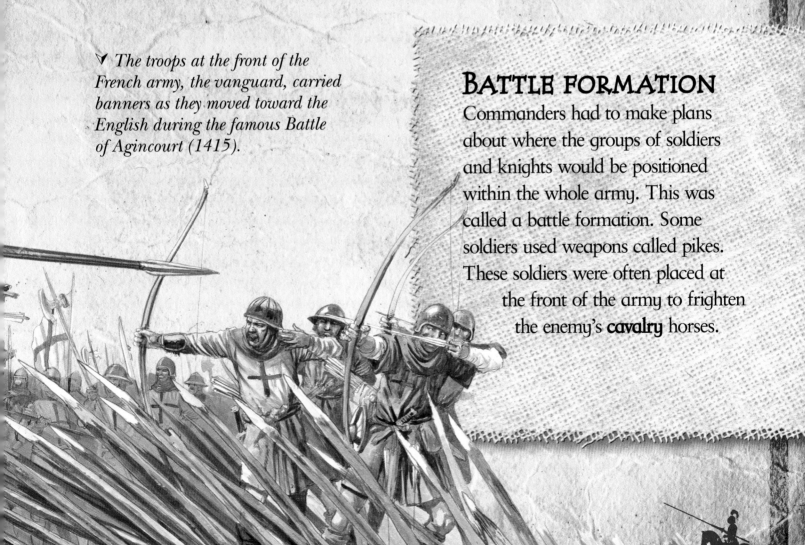

# On the Battlefield

*A good archer could fire more than ten arrows in one minute.*

The medieval battlefield was noisy, and it was often difficult to know who was an enemy and who was a friend. Arrows whistled overhead, often killing soldiers before they even had a chance to fight.

*The English longbowmen attacked the French knights as they approached.*

## HERE COMES THE CAVALRY

In battle, knights rode on horseback in groups called cavalry units. Sometimes they would use a tactic called a cavalry charge, when the knights would ride very fast toward the enemy. As the knights were high up on horses, they could attack enemy foot soldiers. Knights on horseback charging forward could be a terrifying sight.

# THE BATTLE OF AGINCOURT

The Hundred Years War began in 1337 and ended in 1453. It was a war between the English and French over who should rule France. In 1415, the most famous battle in the Hundred Years War took place. This was the Battle of Agincourt. England's king, Henry V, led his soldiers to Agincourt, France. It had rained, and the battlefield was covered in mud. French soldiers became stuck in the mud, making it easier for the English army to attack. Many French soldiers were killed, but fewer English soldiers fell. Henry V won the battle.

# Heralds and Heraldry

$S$ometime around the 1100s, knights began putting symbols on their shields so they could be recognized. These were soon added to coats that knights wore over their armor. The symbols became known as a coat-of-arms. This system of symbols was called heraldry.

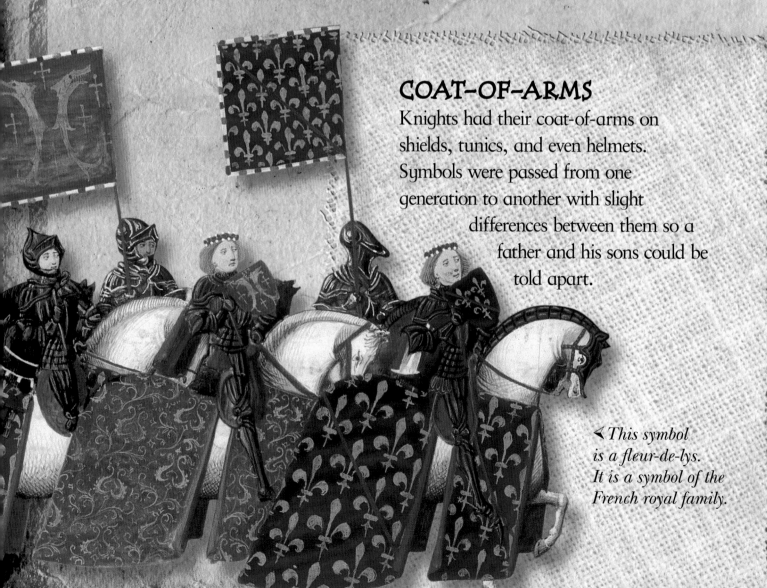

## COAT-OF-ARMS

Knights had their coat-of-arms on shields, tunics, and even helmets. Symbols were passed from one generation to another with slight differences between them so a father and his sons could be told apart.

◁ *This symbol is a fleur-de-lys. It is a symbol of the French royal family.*

# WHO WERE HERALDS?

In jousting tournaments, heralds were in charge of identifying and announcing the knights. Knights also took heralds to battle, where they carried messages from one commander to another. Heralds kept records of knights' coats-of-arms and created the system of heraldry.

▷ *In jousting tournaments, heralds blew horns to signal the start of the competition.*

## Order of the Garter

*The Order of the Garter is the most important honor a knight can be given in England. Today, there are fewer than 30 knights with this title. One of these knights is the Prince of Wales. The order's emblem is a garter with the **motto**, "shame upon him who thinks evil of this" in French. King Edward III started the Order in 1348.*

107

# Castle Under Attack

Castles were the residences of important nobles and the king. They were large because they were built to protect the lord and his family, as well as the local villagers who worked on the land.

## THE FIRST DEFENSES

Some castles were built on hills. Often, a castle had a large **moat**, or ditch, built around it to stop attackers from getting in. A **drawbridge** across the moat made it possible for people to enter the castle. This was lifted up if the castle was under attack.

Battering ram

Crossbowman

Tunnel opening

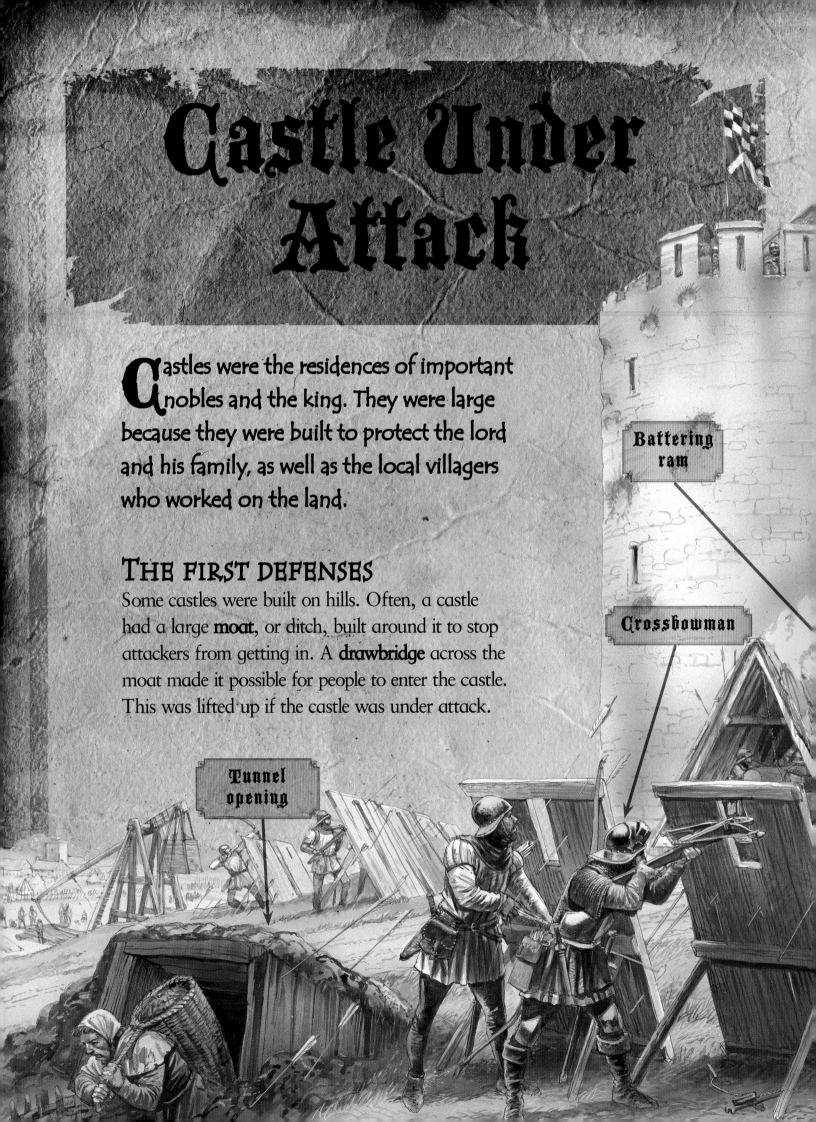

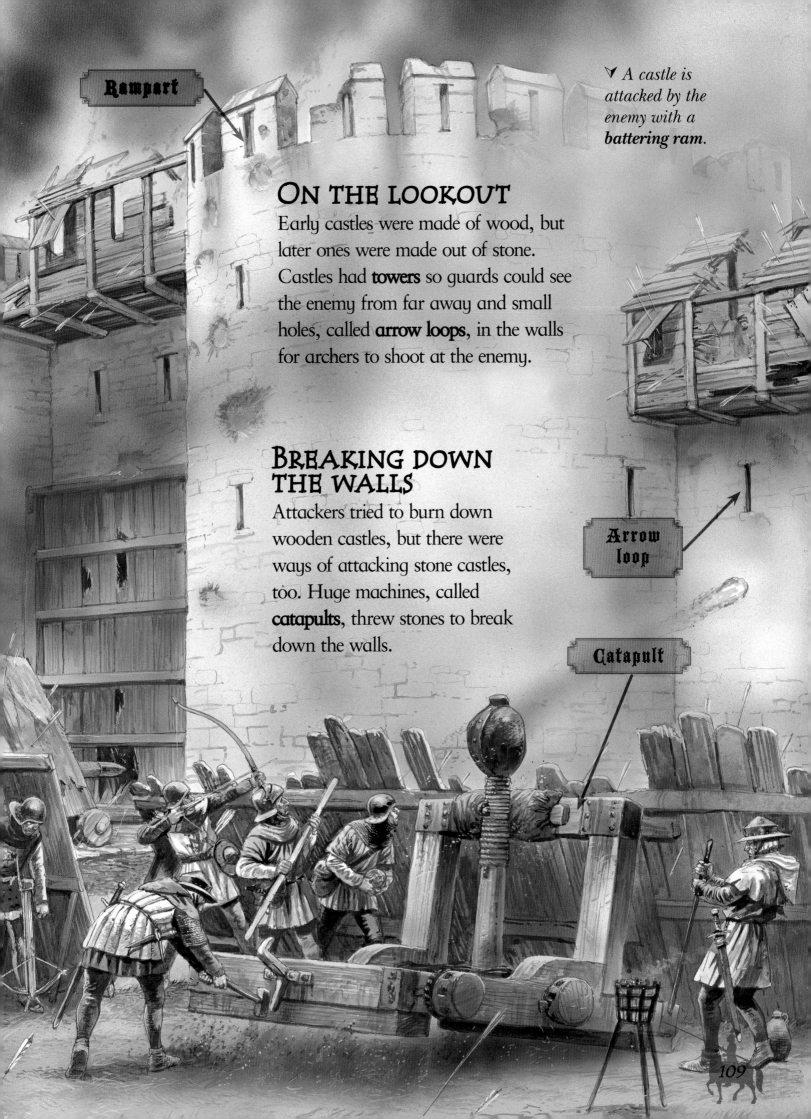

**Rampart**

A castle is attacked by the enemy with a **battering ram**.

## ON THE LOOKOUT

Early castles were made of wood, but later ones were made out of stone. Castles had **towers** so guards could see the enemy from far away and small holes, called **arrow loops**, in the walls for archers to shoot at the enemy.

## BREAKING DOWN THE WALLS

Attackers tried to burn down wooden castles, but there were ways of attacking stone castles, too. Huge machines, called **catapults**, threw stones to break down the walls.

**Arrow loop**

**Catapult**

# Off the Battlefield

All knights had some land or a house to live in when they were not at war. Only the most powerful and noble knights had their own castles.

## CASTLE LIFE

When at home, knights had other people do work for them. They sometimes held large **banquets**, or feasts, in their homes. There were jugglers, acrobats, and **minstrels** to entertain the guests.

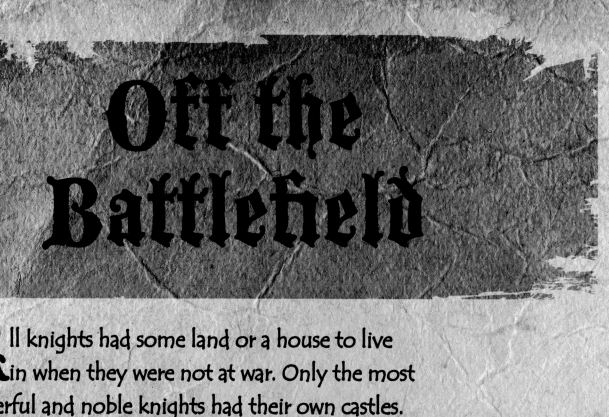

▾ *Banquets in the 1400s involved many different kinds of entertainment.*

# HUNTING AND HAWKING

Knights rode horses to hunt large animals, such as deer or boar, and used dogs to sniff out and chase the animals. Knights and ladies also enjoyed hawking, when they hunted small animals using birds. They would catch a wild bird and train it to kill small animals.

*▽ Stag hunting was seen as a noble sport. Only the most powerful lords and ladies hunted stags.*

## WARRIOR WISDOM

In the Middle Ages, people mostly ate food that was grown or hunted on their land. They also shopped at markets for food that they could not get at home. Markets sold different kinds of food, such as fish.

# Tournaments

When they were not at war, knights held tournaments, or fighting competitions. Tournaments helped knights practice for battle. Soon, these tournaments became a popular form of entertainment.

## PRETEND BATTLES

In each tournament, there were many different events. Mêlées, or pretend battles, were the earliest kind of fighting in a tournament. The knights were separated into two teams. Each team had to try to capture prisoners from the other, but there were very few rules.

▼ *King René of Anjou (1409–1480) enjoyed watching tournaments.*

*Knights used lances in jousting competitions as well as in battle.*

## WARRIOR WISDOM

When Edward I of England fought Scotland and Wales in the 1200s, he had to ban jousting tournaments. Too many of his men were fighting in competitions instead of fighting in the real battles.

## ONE-ON-ONE

Jousting was a battle between two knights. They rode toward each other and tried to knock one another off their horses. If one of the knights succeeded, he was awarded maximum points. Knights also scored points for good fighting skills.

# The Decline of Knights

**T**oward the end of the Middle Ages, knights became less important in battles. Kings began to use paid soldiers, called mercenaries, to fight for them. These soldiers were always ready for battle.

## NEW WEAPONS

In the late Middle Ages, longbows were powerful enough to shoot through plate armor. By the 1300s, cannons and guns had been developed. These new weapons became the strongest force on the battlefield.

*Guns were such powerful weapons that soon knights were no longer needed.*

*Longbows were used to fire arrows at the enemy from a distance.*

# The Knights Templar

The Knights Templar were an order, or group, of knights that stayed in the Middle East after the First Crusade. They set up banks, built castles, and had a huge fleet of ships. In 1312, the Church said that some of the order's beliefs were un-Christian, and their order was banned.

## TRADE

In the 1500s, new routes across land and sea were found. **Merchants** became wealthy by buying and selling goods such as spices and silk— sometimes they were wealthier than a king! Kings made many merchants into knights. By this time, the title of "knight" was just an honor and had nothing to do with fighting.

◀ *Merchant ships traveled all over the world to trade goods.*

# Glossary

**Amphitheater** A round or oval building with seating around a central arena for sporting or entertainment events.

**Archer** A soldier who fights with a bow and arrows.

**Arena** A level area surrounded by seating, in which public events are held.

**Armor** Protective clothing, often made of metal or leather.

**Arrow loop** A narrow slit in a castle wall where archers fired arrows at attackers.

**Banquet** A feast, or meal, for many people.

**Battering ram** A large beam used to break down a wall, door, or gate of a building.

**Battle** A fight between two groups of people.

**Bronze** A yellow-brown metal made of copper and tin.

**Bushi** The class of samurai and their families.

**Bushido** A code of behavior that samurai were supposed to follow.

**Catapult** A machine used to throw objects.

**Cavalry** Soldiers on horseback.

**Chain mail** A kind of armor made of tiny metal rings linked together.

**Chivalry** A code of good behavior that knights were supposed to follow.

**Citizen** A free man in Roman society.

**City-state** A city and the surrounding area that forms an independent state.

**Clan** A group of closely related families.

**Class** A person's position in the community.

**Coat-of-arms** A set of symbols that stand for a person, family, or country.

**Crest** A ridge or plume sticking up from the top of a helmet.

**Crusade** A war in which Christians fought for religious reasons.

**Cuirass** A piece of armor, usually made of bronze that covers the chest.

**Daimyo** The head of a great family in Japan.

**Daisho** The two swords (the katana and wakizashi) that samurai traditionally carried.

**Drawbridge** A bridge over a moat that can be lifted up to stop attackers from getting inside a castle.

**Duel** A fight between two people, usually with swords.

**Eclipse** An event in which some or all of the light from the sun or moon is blocked out by another planetary body.

**Emperor** The ruler of an empire. (see Empire)

**Empire** A large number of states ruled over by a person, a group of people, or another state.

**Equites** Gladiators who fought on horseback.

**Fencing** The practice of sword-fighting.

**Feudal system** A system that orders people depending on how important or powerful they are. A king would be at the top and a peasant would be at the bottom.

**Fresco** A painting made on wet plaster.

**Funeral** A ceremony in which a dead person is buried or cremated.

**Gauntlet** A kind of glove covered in metal.

**General** A leader in an army.

**Government** A group of people who rule a country or state.

**Greave** A kind of armor worn on the leg.

**Heir** A person who has the right to take over the property or position of power from another person once they have died.

**Hellenistic Age** The period in Greek and Asian history between Alexander the Great's death in 323 BC and the rise of Roman power in 146 BC.

**Heraldry** The system of recording the symbols, or coat-of-arms, that knights had.

**Hoplomachi** Gladiators who fought with a sword and spear.

**Javelin** A lightweight spear.

**Jousting tournament** A one-to-one competition in which one knight tried to knock the other off his horse.

**Katana** A long, curved sword that samurai used as a weapon.

**League** A collection of people or countries that work together to help or protect each other against other powers.

**Linen** A thick material, similar to cotton.

**Literature** Written work such as poems.

**Ludus** A kind of school in which gladiators were trained to fight.

**Mask** Something that covers the face to hide it or for protection.

**Mediterranean** The countries around the Mediterranean Sea.

**Mercenary** A soldier who is paid to fight for a foreign country or lord.

**Merchant** Someone who buys and sells goods such as silk, perfume, and fabric.

**Middle Ages** A period that lasted between about AD 500–1500 in Europe.

**Minstrel** A singer or musician.

**Moat** A ditch dug around a castle to help protect it from enemies.

**Monk** A man who is part of a religious group that lives separately from everyone else.

**Monument** A building, statue, or other structure that is often built in memory of something.

**Motto** A phrase that describes the intention or beliefs of a group of people.

**Myrmillones** Gladiators who fought with a sword and shield. They wore a crested helmet.

**Ninjutsu** The art of the ninja warrior.

**Noble** Someone from a powerful or wealthy family. There were different kinds of noble, such as lords, barons, and earls.

**Nobori** The banner of a group of warriors led by a shogun.

**Peasant** A poor person who worked on the land.

**Phalanx** A line formation of soldiers who fought in a tight group with shields overlapping, using spears as weapons.

**Plate armor** A kind of armor made

of plates of metal, shaped to fit around the body.

**Politics** The beliefs and ideas of people about how to rule a country or run a government.

**Provocatores** Gladiators who fought with a sword and shield and wore a helmet with a visor.

**Rampart** A stone wall that protects the castle.

**Rebellion** Resistance against a government or ruler of a nation or state.

**Re-enact** To act out past events.

**Region** An area in a country or state.

**Religion** A form of worship that is practiced according to a kind of belief system.

**Republic** A country or state ruled by a group of people.

**Retiarii** Gladiators who fought with a net and trident.

**Sabaton** Part of a knight's armor that covers the foot.

**Samnes** Gladiators who fought with a short sword and rectangular shield.

**Sarissa** A long spear, with points at both ends, carried by Macedonian soldiers.

**Senator** A member of the council that ruled ancient Rome.

**Serf** A peasant who had to work on a lord's land in return for protection.

**Shogun** A samurai commander.

**Shoku** An iron band with spikes worn on the hand by ninja.

**Siege** An attack on a city or building in which the enemy surrounds it, hoping that those inside will surrender.

**Sling** A weapon made of two cords attached to a pouch, used to throw stones or other objects.

**Souvenir** An object made to remind someone of a particular day or event.

**Spear** A long pole with a sharp tip, used for throwing or stabbing.

**Tactic** A carefully planned action.

**Territory** An area belonging to a particular ruler, government, or state.

**Thraeces** Gladiators who fought with a small, curved sword and small shield.

**Tower** A tall structure built to give a good view of the land around a castle.

**Treaty** An agreement between two groups of people.

**Trident** A kind of three-pronged spear.

**Trireme** An ancient Greek ship with sails and three banks of oars.

**Troops** Soldiers in an army.

**Velites** Gladiators who fought with a spear attached to a long strap.

**Visor** Part of a helmet that can be pulled down to protect the face.

**Wakizashi** A short sword that samurai used as a weapon.

**War** A long period of fighting between different countries, states, or armies. Many battles may be fought in a war.

# Index